by tucker shaw

food photographs *by* leigh beisch **illustrations and atmospheric photographs** *by* jay peter salvas

gentlemen, start your ovens

killer recipes for guys

CHRONICLE BOOKS
SAN FRANCISCO

Library of Congress Cataloging-in-Publication Data available.

ISBN-10: 0-8118-5206-7
ISBN-13: 978-0-8118-5206-7

Manufactured in China.

designed *by* Jay Peter Salvas
food and prop styling *by* George Dolese
This book was typeset in Helvetica Neue 8 / 13
The photographer wishes to thank the photo team that worked with her on this
project, especially Sara Slavin for her amazing props and George Dolese for his
sumptuous food.

Distributed in Canada by Raincoast Books
9050 Shaughnessy Street
Vancouver, British Columbia V6P 6E5

10 9 8 7 6 5 4 3 2 1

Chronicle Books LLC
680 Second Street
San Francisco, California 94107

www.chroniclebooks.com

dedication

This book is for Chris Israel and Doc Willoughby, the two best dining companions I'll ever know.

acknowledgments

All thanks are due to Chronicle Books and everyone there who's had a hand in this project. You better know how much I dig you. Bill LeBlond, Jay Peter Salvas, Amy Treadwell, Carrie Bradley, Doug Ogan, and Tera Killip.

Thanks to Leigh Beisch, who amazed me with her clarity, and to George Dolese, who makes my grandfather's chocolate cake better than I do. Thanks to the whole photo crew.

Thanks to Dan Mandel for his enthusiasm. Thanks to Susan for her advice and for sharing her hangover cure. Thanks to the community of Tinkwig, Pennsylvania, for always leaving a light on for me. Thanks to Alex for being so generous with the wheels. Thanks to Jorge, who makes the best pineapple upside-down cake this side of the Big Island, and to Heather, who makes the best carbonara this side of Lupa. Thanks to Brian Ruehl, wherever he is. Thanks, Dad, for the braces. Thanks, Gram, for the blueberries and love.

A particularly special thank-you to the pigs of the world for the wonderful bacon and other pork products you so amply provide. You will be rewarded in your next life.

Thanks to Irma Rombauer and the Beckers, Mark Bittman, L'Équipe Larousse, Raymond Sokolov, Emeril Lagasse, Lidia Bastianich, Julia Child, Roy Andries de Groot, Harold McGee, Alton Brown, Judy Rodgers, Alice Waters, Jacques Pépin, Martin Yan, Two Hot Tamales and Two Fat Ladies, Jamie Oliver, Nigella Lawson, Mario Batali, Eileen Yin-Fei Lo, Rachael Ray, Andreas Viestad, Fletcher Pratt, Robeson Bailey, and a bunch of other people who don't know me from Adam but who have everything to do with why I care about writing about food.

Eternal thanks to Edouard de Pomiane, the best cookbook writer of all time and quite likely the smartest person who ever lived.

table of contents

introduction 06

C06: supper 118

C07: dessert 162

Introduction

men should cook

I believe that every man should know how to cook.

I believe that every man should know how to sauté a steak and create a buttery sauce from the pan. He should be able to purchase and prepare fish. He should know how to fix pancakes and bacon for the whole house. He should know how to produce a birthday cake, because one day there'll be a child or a girl or a good friend in his life who needs one. A well-rounded man is always a good cook.

But besides that, men should also *want* to cook. After all, food matters. It's one of this planet's marquee experiences, right up there with sex and music and love. Men should be all over it. Many men know this already.

This book is for men (and women) like me, who eat without prejudice. We dig fast food, but we love high dinners, too. We savor a diner cheeseburger just as much as foie gras. We believe that junk food and haute cuisine belong in the same belly. We like classic, familiar dishes with strong flavors, but we're not afraid to reach out and try new things. Most of all, we know what we want, and we're willing to put forth a little effort to get it.

Like the old saying: If you want something done right, do it yourself. That's exactly how I feel about meatballs.

In this book you'll find clear, simple recipes for delicious food, most of it food that you already recognize. Not every recipe is easy, but none are all that hard, either. If you can read and follow directions, you can cook the recipes in this book.

None of these recipes require any weird equipment. You don't need a standing mixer if you've got arms. You don't need a state-of-the-art convection oven. You don't even need a grill. (In fact, there are no grilling recipes in this book, because I don't have a grill in my apartment, and it's a ticketable offense to light up your hibachi on the roof. Trust me, I know.) I mention a food processor once or twice, but it's not ultimately necessary if you've got a knife.

With this book you can turn out killer dishes without all of that stuff anyway, and have a good time doing it, even in a scrappy little kitchen like mine.

kitchen hack

Some lucky men learned how to cook from their families. They can navigate naturally and easily around the kitchen, producing flawless meals without even thinking. These men spent long stretches of their youth in the kitchen and at the dining table (whether they wanted to or not) watching and learning about ingredients, meals, and the rhythms of food preparation. But not everyone grows up a Bastianich or a Pépin. In fact, my early years were gastronomically bleak. I only really learned about cooking because I decided, after I'd grown up, that I wanted to know how.

I say this because some think that cooking is somehow magical, that you either can or you can't, that you're either born with it or not. But the truth is, all it takes to be a great cook is to learn how. Anyone who wants to, can.

I'm not a cook by trade and I've had just seven days of formal cooking training: four at the Culinary Institute of America, where I took a basic cooking-methods course, and three days at the Institute of Culinary Education here in New York, where I learned a couple of things about stocks and sauces. But that's about it with the paid lessons.

Just about everything else that I know I learned from books, magazines, friends, and especially TV. Sure, by osmosis my grandparents taught me a couple of important things, such as how to work fast to make a decent pie crust, and how to add hot water to gingerbread dough to give it a moister texture, and how to bread-and-bake a dish of scallops. I have a boatload of friends who kick ass in the kitchen, and I learn from them every time we eat together, which is all the time.

But most of my knowledge, as wide or limited as it may be, comes from reading, watching, and listening to everything from my *Larousse Gastronomique* to *Iron Chef* to

epicurious.com—and then picking up a knife, firing up the oven, and trying it myself.

If I read or see something that looks good, I'll try to make it. In fact, most of my free time is given over to experimenting in the kitchen. I remind myself of my father, who while I was growing up would be in the garage most weekends, all weekend, tinkering with his '67 Firebird convertible (or was it the '64 Oldsmobile coupe?) and emerging only for a stack of baloney sandwiches (white bread, yellow cheese, and Miracle Whip). I'm the same way, now, tinkering, only I'm doing it in the kitchen. And I'll emerge not for food, but *with* food: a *tres leches* cake or a kielbasa frittata or a hot fudge sundae.

There are wide-open, even embarrassing, holes in my skills. I haven't perfected my sabayon, I can't flawlessly debone a chicken, and my peanut brittle is consistently cloudy. But the trend is up, and I know more today than I did yesterday.

Does that make me just a hack in the kitchen? Maybe so. But give a hack a knife, some fire, and an idea, and eventually he'll figure something out.

01

storm th

it's your kitchen. get in there.

First things first: You have to enter, and possess, your kitchen. That means standing around in it, taking stock, getting the lay of the land. Sure, some guys look at it only as a glorified beer-storage unit or a place to unwrap takeout meals and collect garbage. Some guys look at it as just a girl-zone, or something that always needs cleaning. But some of us see our kitchens and think: workshop.

It doesn't matter if your kitchen sucks. It just matters if it works. Take my kitchen, for example. It's small, old, and creaky, and it's crowded, even when it's just me. It has zero ventilation and no dishwasher. It's four floors up, no elevator. The "self-lighting" stove requires a match. The faucet dribbles. There's hardly any storage. *(Did I mention there's no dishwasher?)*

But it works, my little old kitchen, and I love it like an old T-shirt. It does what I ask it to *(even if sometimes it needs an extra nudge)*. I keep it clean and busy, which is all any kitchen wants, really.

four cardinal rules of cooking

There may be more rules in the official rulebook *(whatever* that *is)*, but if you keep these four things sacred, you'll rule the kitchen.

be prepared

The best lesson I ever learned about cooking is the concept of *mise en place.*

It's French that means something to the effect of "Have your shit together before you start."

In other words, read through the recipe, from beginning to end. *(This is an essential step.)* Get out all the ingredients you'll need. Preheat the oven if you need to. Put water on to boil if you'll need it later. Have within reach all the tools required. Prepare any pans that need greasing or flouring. Know what order you're going to do things in. Take a second and visualize the process. This minimizes surprises and the chances of being caught unprepared. It's important–stopping mid-sear to search for the tongs can be deadly to your steak or fish, and you paid good money for it.

timing is everything

Serving temperature is just as important to your food as flavor and appearance. Your spinach should never wait for your steak. When you make something you want to serve hot, serve it hot. If it's a cold dish, serve it cold. Just make sure that you get things on the table the way you like them. If you're haphazard about it, you'll be disappointed.

This plays into the whole *mise en place* thing, because it's about planning and timing. You want everything that you're preparing to be ready at the right time. So make sure your plates and bowls are ready, the glasses filled, and the salt is on the table when it's time to eat.

make extra

Leftovers are one of the great joys of life. Many dishes, like stews and chili and lemon cake, taste better the second day, and even better on the third. So make extra of dishes like these, and hang on to them for lunch tomorrow. Also, think about sandwiches whenever you're making a snack or meal. If it sounds like it might taste good on a sandwich *(and most things do)*, then make extra to put in a sandwich down the line.

think about your health

I'm not a huge advocate of any kind of dieting or any of that stuff. But I will tell you this: When you cook for yourself, you eat more healthfully. When you pick out your own ingredients, you have a lot more control. So besides being good, cooking at home makes for a healthier diet, too. Enough said.

stuff to have

The following is a big old list of everything I have in my kitchen. It could be a pretty good guide for what you should have, too. You don't need all this stuff to make the recipes in this book. In fact, you could hack together 85 percent of the recipes in here with just a knife, cutting board, tongs, a bowl, and an ovenproof sauté pan. But while I'd never, ever advocate an overequipped kitchen, it is nice to have a few extra toys in the box.

KNIVES AND BLADES

- 1 **heavy chef's knife**, 10 inches
- 1 **dimpled chef's knife**, 9 inches
- 1 **paring knife**
- 1 **serrated bread knife**
- 1 set of **all-purpose kitchen scissors** for herbs and bacon
- 1 set of **poultry shears**
- 1 **knife sharpening steel**
- 1 **plastic cutting board** *(I throw it away every 4 or 5 months and get a new one)*
- 1 **wooden cutting board**

POTS AND PANS

- 2 **heavy ovenproof sauté pans ***; one 10 inches in diameter, one 7 inches in diameter for omelets
- 1 **medium cast-iron frying pan**, 11 inches in diameter

*WTF is a sauté pan, you may ask? Call it a frying pan or a skittle or whatever you want. It's all shades of gray, really, especially for the recipes in this book. Some pans *(called* sauteurs *in French)* have straight perpendicular sides, and are better for frittatas and cornbread. Others *(called* sauteuses *in French, or typically "frying pans" around here)* have sloped sides and are better for eggs. Experiment. In this book, I usually say "sauté pan," but if that annoys you, just insert "frying pan."

1 large, enamel-coated cast-iron **Dutch oven**, 8 quarts

1 large **soup pot** for soups and pasta

1 **medium saucepan**, 3 to 4 quarts

1 **small saucepan**, 3 cups

1 metal **vegetable steamer**

2 large, heavy **baking sheets**

One 9-by-13-inch **baking pan**

Two 9-inch **round cake pans**

One 8- or 9-inch **square cake pan**

Two 9-inch **pie dishes**

1 **pizza stone**

1 heavy **roasting pan** with rack

2 **wire cooling racks**

BOWLS

2 **large mixing bowls**

2 **medium mixing bowls**

2 **small mixing bowls**

TOOLS AND GADGETS

1 **can opener**

1 **churchkey**

1 **corkscrew**

2 **bottle stoppers**

1 pair **tongs**

1 **slotted spoon**

1 large **metal spoon**

2 favorite **wooden spoons**; one for savory dishes, one for sweet stuff

1 **whisk**

1 wooden handheld **citrus juicer**

1 **vegetable peeler**

1 **ladle**

1 rubber **spatula/spoon** thing (*I think they call it a spoonula*)

1 **metal spatula**

1 **flexible offset spatula** (*long, skinny spatula that can easily wedge itself under pie pieces or fish fillets without tearing them up*)

1 **Microplane grater**

1 **box grater-shredder**

1 **nutmeg grater**

1 **brush** with synthetic, heatproof bristles for brushing on glazes and marinades

1 **marble mortar and pestle** for grinding spices and nuts

1 **wooden rolling pin** made of a solid piece of wood, no sockets or ball bearings

DRAINING AND STRAINING DEVICES

2 large fine-mesh **sieves**; one for sweet things, one for savory

1 **colander**

1 crank-powered **food mill**

1 **salad spinner**

MEASURING STUFF

1 set **measuring spoons**

1 set **dry measuring cups**

1 small Pyrex **liquid measuring cup**, 2 cups

1 large Pyrex **liquid measuring cup**, 4 cups

TEMPERATURE STUFF

1 **oven thermometer** (*essential, because the chances that your oven thermometer reading and the actual temperature in your oven are the same are, well, slim at best*)

1 **instant-read thermometer** to make sure meats are cooked through (*thus avoiding a whole host of food poisonings and the like*)

1 **candy thermometer** (*not necessary unless you're making candy, but fun to screw around with anyway*)

DISPOSABLE STUFF

A few **Tupperware containers** in various sizes, replaced once per year

2 rolls of heavy-duty **aluminum foil**

2 boxes of **Ziploc bags**, small and big

2 rolls **parchment paper**

1 roll **plastic wrap**

APPLIANCES

1 **handheld blender** (*also called an immersion blender, which lets you puree things right in the pot*)

1 **stand blender** (*for blending sauces, soups, and, most importantly, margaritas*)

1 large **food processor**

1 **electric handheld mixer**

1 small **microwave oven**

THINGS I HAVE THAT I NEVER USE

1 electric **citrus juicer**

1 standing **tapered sieve**

1 **mini food processor** (*some people swear by these, but I just think it's a pain in the neck to clean*)

1 **turkey baster**

THINGS I WISH I HAD

Wok and **accessories**

Springform cake pan for cheesecakes and other cakes that I still need to learn how to make

Mandoline (*a special tool with a really sharp blade for cutting vegetables extra-thin*)

A **standing mixer** (*by the time you read this, I've likely invested in one*)

Fry Daddy

So that's what I have (*and don't have*), and I'd say it's a pretty good checklist for figuring out what you should have, too.

a few words about your knives

Pretty much everyone who cooks a lot, pro or am, will say the same thing: Their knives are their most important piece of equipment. I concur. I love my chef's knife. It's worn but shiny-new all at once. It's from Japan and has a killer edge and always looks great on that magnetic strip I have bolted to the wall.

A good knife is made from a single piece of metal that runs all the way through the handle. If you have a blade attached to a handle with no carryover, you have a lame knife. It should be heavy and it should fit comfortably in your hand. The edge should be sharp enough to make you respect it. You should expect to spend $100 or so for a slamming chef's knife, but it will last forever if you take care of it. Spend the money and don't skimp.

Each time you cook, you should give your knife a few strokes along the finest side of your sharpening blade. If you don't have a sharpening blade, you should get one. Go to a finer kitchen store and ask them to demonstrate for you how to use it. Practice with them until you get the motion down. It's very simple once you learn it, and it will keep your knife blade plenty sharp from day to day.

Every six months, however, your knife needs a visit to a professional to correct microscopic nicks and straighten and hone the edge and tip. This is the same schedule you should be on for the dentist, so find a knife sharpener near your dentist and drop it off for him to sharpen while your teeth are being cleaned. Just a suggestion.

Another, better, suggestion would be to learn how to sharpen your own knives, using a sharpening stone. But be sure to learn from someone who really knows what they're doing, or you'll damage your knives on the stone.

Store your knives in a knife block or on a magnet. Do not toss your knife in a drawer, where the blade will knock up against a bunch of stuff that will dull it. Do not toss it in the sink, either, where it will end up nicked and roughed up. Don't **ever** put your knives in the dishwasher.

Serrated knives, indispensable for bread, and dimpled knives, which aren't required but do help when chopping things like onions, also require careful storage and regular visits to the sharpener.

Remember that a heavy, sharp knife is actually safer than a dull or light one, because it doesn't slide off the food and onto your finger. Which is good 'cause you didn't want that finger in your salad, did you?

Treat your knife well and you'll be together forever.

a few words about your pots and pans

Spend some money and buy high-quality pots and pans. This means they should be heavy, especially the bottoms, with sturdy handles and tight-fitting lids.

Good pots and pans will last forever. Make sure you trust the salesperson you're working with, and get the finest quality you can afford. Poorly made pots and pans don't conduct heat well, and your food burns. So buy good ones.

Consider an aluminum core with a stainless surface. That combo works well for me, with even heat conductivity and a noncorrosive finish. But some people swear by copper core. Also, I prefer a stainless surface to a black one, because I feel like I can see what's happening in the pan better, but some people like the black surface. I suppose that one is your call.

You don't need the fourteen-piece suite, just a sauté pan, a couple of saucepans, and a couple of baking pans and sheets. And a good, heavy, enamel-covered Dutch oven, like those made by Le Creuset, is like a piece of magic, making any braise or stew or soup sing in a way that straight metal pots just won't do. (Plus they're easier to clean.)

Cast-iron pans are great for everyday bacon and eggs, and they get better with time. If you can get your hands on an old, well-seasoned pan, do it. If it's seasoned, it'll be, for all intents and purposes, nonstick. Plus they say it imparts iron into the food you're eating, which is only good for you. If you buy yourself a new one, it should come with instructions for how to season it. The best way I've found is to coat the inside with Crisco, then heat up the pan as hot as it will get, then let it sit and cool, then wipe it clean. Some people suggest rubbing the Crisco in with salt, which I suppose won't hurt, but seems unnecessary. Never, ever use soap on a seasoned cast-iron pan, or it will lose its near nonstick surface. Just rinse with water, wipe clean, and dry thoroughly to prevent rusting.

the well-stocked fridge (and cupboard)

I've always thought that cooking a meal is like directing a film. And isn't directing really 90 percent casting? Same with cooking: It's 90 percent ingredients. So buy the best (see page 19–20) and take care of them. I guarantee that your meals will be better for it.

Also, remember that recipes are never the last word. At best, they're starting points and inspiration. I'm not always able to follow a recipe straight through. I usually get sidetracked into one variation or another along the way, as my mind wanders with my eye around the kitchen to find ways to enhance or alter. It's about having a plan, but having the flexibility and fearlessness to make something your own, hopefully for the better. And it's about having good ingredients to work with on hand.

Here are the staples you should have in your fridge and cupboard. (Note: I'm not going to include in this list such necessities as Cool Whip, beef jerky, and Fudgsicles. Whatever your snack foods are, you're in charge there.) This should cover the basics of what you need for pretty much any recipe in this book, although you'll have to buy things like meat and bread and most produce as you need them. They need to be fresh when you use them.

BACK WALL

The back wall of your fridge is the coolest spot. Use this VIP area for important stuff that needs to stay really cold. Never store butter in the butter dish on the door.

Bacon

Butter

Chicken stock

Cheese

Eggs

Milk

Yogurt

IN THE CRISPER

Believe it or not, the crisper is an aptly named feature of your fridge. It really does help keep things crisp.

Carrots

Celery

Green onions

Lettuces and other greens like **spinach**

Seasonal **fruits** and **vegetables**

ON THE SHELVES

Anchovies

Ketchup *(Heinz. Skip the boutique-y stuff.)*

Mayonnaise *(Hellmann's, please. Miracle Whip, while delicious, is not mayonnaise.)*

Mustard *(both smooth Dijon and country/whole-grain)*

Olives

Red peppers in a jar *(sometimes called roasted, sometimes marinated, but they amount to essentially the same thing . . . try a few brands until you find your favorite)*

Wedge of **Parmesan** *(buy Parmigiano-Reggiano if you can . . . and always grate it as you go, because pre-grated cheese tastes like pre-grated cardboard within a couple of days)*

DOWN LOW

Beer

Leftovers

Soda

ON THE DOOR

Batteries

Hot pepper sauces *(I keep a selection around, some Mexican, some Asian, some Caribbean)*

Water

White wine

IN THE FREEZER

Frozen meat

Frozen stock *(see page 108)*

Ice cream

Popsicles

Tequila *(not vodka, as it makes the martinis too gooey)*

OUT OF THE FRIDGE

Avocados *(don't keep these in the fridge or they'll turn into concrete)*

Bananas

Garlic

Ginger

Lemons

Limes

Shallots

Yellow onions

Potatoes

IN THE CUPBOARD

Beans, canned *(red and white and black)*

Beans, dried *(red and white, and lentils and split peas if you like those)*

Broth, canned or boxed *(chicken and beef)*

Clam juice

Couscous

Egg noodles

Maple syrup

Olive oil

Pasta in various shapes, short and long

Rice *(and any other grains you dig, like bulgur or barley, which are easy to prepare and, with enough butter, delicious)*

Red wine

Tomatoes, canned *(whole and crushed . . . buy imported Italian ones because they're better)*

Tomato paste *(in cans or in a tube)*

Assorted vinegars *(red wine, white wine, regular white distilled, balsamic)*

BAKING STUFF

(change every 6 months for potency)

Baking powder

Baking soda

Brown sugar

All-purpose flour

Granulated sugar

Powdered sugar

Sweetened condensed milk

Vanilla extract *(make sure it's pure)*

DRIED HERBS AND SPICES

(change every few months, or at least once a year, for potency)

Bay leaves

Black peppercorns and grinder

Celery seed

Chile powders

Ground **cinnamon**

Dried minced onions

Dried cumin

Dried herbs *(thyme, oregano, sage, whichever you like)*

Dry mustard

Whole **nutmeg** and grater

Garlic powder

Red pepper flakes

SALTS

Kosher

Old-school **table salt**

Sea

(Kosher is best for cooking, table salt for baking and dissolving. Sea salt is great on the table for salads and meats.)

hidden arsenal

Building flavors sometimes means adding hidden support. Here are a few killer flavor enhancers. You'll find them in your well-stocked kitchen.

ANCHOVIES

Far from adding a fishy flavor, anchovies add an earthy, ocean-y saltiness to any dish they're sautéed into, especially soups, stews, and pasta sauce. Most people think they don't like anchovies, but actually do.

BACON

Start stews, meats, soups, and salads with bacon, and already you've raised the stakes in your dish. One piece of bacon, or the fat rendered from it, can add a whole layer of unidentifiable richness to any soup, without being noticeable.

CLAM JUICE

Cooking with fish? Add a little bottled clam juice to your cooking liquid. Cooking with it adds a fresh, ocean-like quality (not a fishy one) to your fish or vegetable dish. Especially good in stews.

KETCHUP

I use ketchup in soups, stews, pasta sauces, chili, meat loaf, and many other dishes. It's got a ready-balanced blend of flavors spanning sweet to tart to salty, which gives a smooth finish to whatever you add it to. Don't use too much, and don't add it to anything that it'll overpower.

MAYONNAISE

Add a tablespoon of mayo to your warm hashbrowns, and you'll be a believer. While homemade mayo isn't that hard to make and is a real pleasure, Hellmann's mayonnaise has a quality that is not re-creatable. Smooth and rich without being too heavy, it's a great addition to salad dressings. Just keep it simple and small, no more than a teaspoon in a ½ cup of dressing.

MUSTARD

Three kinds of mustard live in my kitchen: smooth Dijon, country style (wholegrain), and dry. Also, there's a squeeze bottle of yellow mustard for hot dogs, but I don't often cook with it. Mustard adds a vinegary, spicy, slightly floral and fresh note to meats, vegetables, soups, stews, and more.

NUTMEG

Nutmeg is a flavor familiar to anyone who smells it, but people often have to be reminded about it. Just a few gratings of this strong-scented nut will add an otherwise-unattainable finish to baked goods, fish, and many vegetables.

storing leftovers

The key to storing leftovers is to reduce the amount of air they come into contact with. It's hard to beat heavy-duty aluminum foil and containers with tight-fitting lids like Tupperware. Wrapping a piece of plastic over a plate is a no-go. One good way to store food is in a nonreactive (usually glass) bowl, with aluminum foil tightly pressed down on the surface of the food.

When you're refrigerating leftovers, make sure to get them in the fridge within a couple of hours. Don't put anything in there hot, but if leftovers sit at room temperature too long, you're asking for problems downstairs.

Most leftovers keep for about three to five days. Some, like stew and chili and meats, actually get tastier with age. Others, like bread and cake, start to lose their appeal. Don't eat anything that has a funny color, and if you're not sure, err on the side of safety and toss it.

shop like you mean it

Simple equation: The better your ingredients, the better your cooking. If you can't afford the best, get the best you can afford. It's worth it.

To be a great shopper you have to first establish a relationship with a butcher *(this may take a few visits, but be persistent)* and a fish vendor. If you can get access to fresh butter, milk, and eggs, invest in it. Figure out where your local farmers' market happens, and go every week to stock up on fruits and vegetables. Find specialty shops for imported ingredients like anchovies or fresh-baked bread. Shop around until you find your favorites. Sometimes it's the finest shop in town, but sometimes your favorites come from the local Circle K.

But be realistic, too. You don't want to be chasing food all day every day. Our hunter-gatherer ancestors did that for millions of years so that we don't have to. If your community has a nice, big grocery store that does a lot of business, it's good enough for most things.

One thing that really pays off is using coupons and shopping for specials. I spend ten minutes every Sunday going through the coupons. There are always two or three things I'll need, like cleaning products or condiments. I've never audited myself, but I bet I save 10 percent on groceries over the course of the year, and that's not for nothing. Just make sure that whatever you're stocking up on isn't too perishable.

dairy

If you can get fresh butter from a local dairy and you can afford it, go for it. Have at least a pound on hand, and make sure it's unsalted, so that *you* control the salt in your final dish. As for milk, choose whole and/or 2 percent. Skim is fine for drinking, if you're into that, but it doesn't much work for cooking. Get some yogurt, 'cause it's a good snack, and don't leave without ice cream. If you're baking and you'll need it, grab some buttermilk.

eggs

The best eggs are always from the farmers' market; get organic, free-range eggs, the freshest you can find. Avoid the plain old run-of-the-mill eggs your supermarket offers up and buy the good ones if you can. They make a big difference both in eating and in cooking. But if you have only the plain old eggs, they're fine, too.

vegetables

Buy as many vegetables as you can at a farmers' market. Buy what's in season. A couple of trips to the market will clue you in to what's in season. Gorge on tomatoes in summer, squash in the fall. Always have on hand yellow onions, shallots, garlic, potatoes, carrots, and celery. Buy spinach

and other leafy greens, broccoli, aspara-
gus, peppers, and other produce once or
twice a week, as you need it. Same with
fresh herbs like basil, parsley, and sage.
If you're not sure whether what's in your
fridge is still good, buy fresh.

fruit

As with vegetables, all you need to remember
is to eat in season. Berries in the summer,
apples in the fall, oranges in the winter. Buy
most fruit slightly underripe to give you a
few days to get to it. Always buy lemons
and limes.

meat

Do your best to have a conversation with the
butcher whenever you buy meat. Most
high-end grocery stores have a butcher on
site. You don't have to make friends with
him like they do on all those cooking shows,
but at least exchange a word or two. Let
him know what you're looking for and what
you're going to do with it. It's likely he's
an incredible cook himself and will have
good tips. If you don't have access to
a butcher, look for date stamps on meat
to ensure freshness. Beef should be red,
never gray. Pork is pinker, but also not gray.
Chicken should be clean with firm, pale
flesh, not bloody and yellowing. Always pick
up a pound of slab bacon.

fish

Buy fish the day you're going to use it. As
with meat, it pays to talk your plans over
with the fish guy and get the freshest you
can find. It should smell like the ocean (never
like fish) and it should have a uniform
color. If you're buying a whole fish, check
that the eyes are nice and clear. Shellfish
should have shells firmly closed. Buy shrimp
in the shell, and prepare them yourself.

baking products

Check for freshness dates wherever you
can, and don't buy the biggest bag of flour
there is. You'll never use it before it loses
its freshness. Have on hand 5-pound bags
of flour and sugar, fresh baking powder
and baking soda, and some high-quality
real (labeled "pure") vanilla extract, and
you're good.

other staples

Always stock up on tortillas because they're
delicious. Make sure you have enough
mustard, ketchup, and mayonnaise on hand.
Know if you need olive oil, vinegar, chicken
stock, beans, rice, and pasta, or any spices.
Cake mixes or cornbread mixes are good
to have around, as is pancake or biscuit mix.
So is cereal, which is what I buy more
of than anything else. As to snacks and
munchies—it's all you.

specialty items

There are some things for which you'll
probably need a specialty store like an Asian,
Mexican, or Italian market, or at least a
gourmet grocery store with dedicated depart-
ments. They include:

Imported **canned tomatoes,
anchovies,** and **olives**

Imported **fish sauce, kimchee,**
and other international **condiments**

Dried spices like **curry powders,
cumin,** and the whole range of **dried
smoked chiles**

Fresh bread

Better cheeses

and don't forget

Plenty of cleaning products and paper towels. And what the hell, treat yourself to a new sponge.

When you get your groceries home, put them away immediately. Rachael Ray says to wash all of your produce before putting it away so it's clean when you need it. I completely concur.

clean this

It's good to have a clean kitchen. Luckily it doesn't take that much work. There are only two rules.

The number-one rule of a clean kitchen is: Cook first, clean later. Your kitchen is about cooking, not cleaning. Don't ever let a potential mess keep you from cooking or improvising in the kitchen. You're going to make a mess whether you like it or not, so just go for it. You'll deal with the mess later.

The number-two rule of a clean kitchen is: Be consistent. Ten minutes of effort at the end of the night is all it takes to always have a clean kitchen. OK, maybe twenty, if you really trashed the place. In ten minutes you can get the dishes out of the way, wipe down the countertops and appliances, and get in a quick sweep or Swiff of the floor. Ten minutes is less time than it takes Lynyrd Skynyrd to get through "Freebird."

Once each week or so, spend an extra fifteen minutes on a Saturday morning and clean a little harder than usual. Consider it an investment in your social life, because if you don't have a clean kitchen, no one will want to stay over.

(Full disclosure: Even I don't live up to all the suggestions I've laid out here. But I do my best, and for the best kitchen, you should too.)

dishes

If you've got a dishwasher, run it at the end of each day, if it's half full or fuller. Don't run it in the morning because that's when everyone's trying to get in a decent shower and when it comes to water pressure, people come before dishes.

If you don't have a dishwasher, do the dishes before you go to bed. You have to. If you leave dirty dishes out, you'll have food-crusted plates, not to mention mice if you're really unlucky. Use very hot water and plenty of detergent. If the water's too hot for your hands, which it should be, put your balls in your purse and slip on a pair of dishwashing gloves. Wash your cutting boards along with your dishes with very hot water and detergent.

Keep kitchen towels clean *(always start with a fresh one)*, and change your sponge once every couple of weeks or so.

Empty the drain trap in your sink, and finish with a sink wipe.

countertop

God only knows what you've been doing on the countertops. Wipe them down with a spritz of kitchen cleaner and a couple paper towels at the end of the day. Check the bases and cases of any appliances you used, like the blender base.

21

Once every few months, sand and oil your wooden cutting boards. Twice a year, toss and replace plastic cutting boards.

oven

If you don't clean your oven, all of your food will start to taste the same: Burnt.

If you've got a self-cleaning oven, fire it up every couple of months. If you don't have a self-cleaning oven, like I don't, get out the oven cleaner every two to three months. It's easy. First, open the windows, because it smells awful. Then, spray it on all of the oven surfaces. Rinse your hands, grab a bag of Fritos, and go watch TV. The cleaner bubbles away in your oven while you loaf. After half an hour, return to wipe it out with a few paper towels. Done. Don't forget the broiler.

Once every couple of weeks, give the inside of your microwave a quick wipe with some kitchen cleaner and paper towels.

stove top

After dinner, wipe down the stove top with an antibacterial kitchen cleaner and a paper towel, scrubbing up any cooked-on food so it doesn't become a permanent feature. Once a week, clean under the elements or burner grates if you have them.

hood

If you have a hood, follow your manufacturer's instructions to keep it clean.

refrigerator

Refrigerators are like restaurants: The higher the turnover, the fresher the food. So, turn it over. Every couple of weeks open up the fridge and take a look. Toss the expired stuff and anything you can't identify. Check vegetables. Cheese, which I am unlikely to have because I probably ate it already, should be free of any visible mold.

Use last-chance vegetables in a kitchen-cupboard pasta sauce or soup.

Check the fridge for spills. Every six months, clear it out completely, defrost the freezer, and wipe down the inside, including the crisper drawers, with kitchen cleaner and some paper towels. If your fridge isn't clean, your butter will smell like leftovers and beer.

walls

Walls pick up odors from steam and smoke, not to mention the occasional splatter. No need to go insane on them; if you wipe them down quickly about once a month, your place won't smell like garlic and fish. Once a year, give them a thorough wash with soap and water. Every three years or so, repaint.

floor

Sweep or Swiff the floor every couple of days. This doesn't take long and is better than stepping on a soggy tortilla chip when you're barefoot. If you've spilled anything wet or potentially sticky, wipe it up right away. Every week or so, break out the mop and give the floor a wet wash. If it's a wood floor, hit it with a little wood-floor cleaner.

02

all day b

breakfast. is it really just breakfast?

Some people define breakfast as the morning meal, the first meal of the day, coming once each morning, sometime between waking up and lunchtime. I think those people are shortsighted and probably secretly unhappy.

Because breakfast is too good to box in.

Like, it's still breakfast, even if you don't get to it until the afternoon, as was the case with me last Sunday. *(Don't judge.)* And who's to say you can't have lunch when you first wake up, and breakfast later? And for that matter, why can't you have breakfast two or three times in a day?

I'm all for free and easy breakfast, all day long. Even for dinner.

And I'm not the only one. As every diner owner worth his hash browns knows, breakfast foods are the most popular thing on the menu, no matter what time of day it is.

reakfast

serves **2**

huevos rancheros sandwiches on toasted spicy cornbread

I like Mexican food for breakfast, lunch, and dinner. Not that this is some kind of authentic Mexican dish; actually, it's pretty gringo in a lot of ways. But who cares? It's good. If you don't feel like putting in the ten minutes of effort it takes to make your own cornbread *(lame)*, you can make these with thick white bread or sourdough or something like that.

FOR THE **SPICY CORNBREAD**

Unsalted butter for greasing the pan

1 box **cornbread mix** *(I like Jiffy Corn Muffin mix, which can be used for cornbread as well. If you've got no mix in the pantry, combine 1 cup corn meal, ½ cup all-purpose flour, 2 tablespoons sugar, 1 teaspoon baking powder, ½ teaspoon baking soda, and ½ teaspoon salt.)*

1 large **egg,** at room temperature, lightly beaten

¾ cup **buttermilk**

½ teaspoon **lemon juice**

1 teaspoon **red pepper flakes,** finely crushed between your thumb and forefinger *(don't rub your eyes after crushing them)*

2 tablespoons **vegetable oil**

FOR THE **SANDWICHES**

4 slabs **cornbread** *(recipe at left)*

Unsalted butter for spreading, plus 2 tablespoons for frying

1 cup shredded **Cheddar cheese,** plus extra for garnish *(also good: queso fresco or pepper Jack)*

4 large **eggs**

Leaves of 1 small bunch fresh **cilantro,** chopped

Hot sauce *(You'll find several of these in your fridge. Close your eyes and pick one.)*

Coarse **salt** and **pepper**

continued

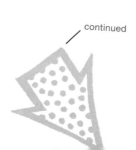

make the cornbread

Preheat the oven to 425°F. Butter a 9-inch-square baking pan. In a medium bowl, combine all the cornbread ingredients until just moistened, pour into the pan, and bake for 20 to 25 minutes, or until the bread is cracked on top, brown on the edges, and pulling away from the pan. Let cool in the pan for 10 minutes, then turn out onto a wire rack. When completely cool, slice into ½-inch slabs. *(Cornbread can be made a day in advance. If it dries out a little, just add more cheese and salsa.)*

make the sandwiches

Using the broiler, toast both sides of the cornbread slabs until lightly browned. Keep your eye on them and do not let them burn. Spread one side of each slab with butter, then sprinkle the cheese over two of the buttered slabs. Return the cheesy slabs to the broiler until the cheese is just beginning to melt, about 1 minute. Remove immediately.

Over high heat, melt the 2 tablespoons butter in a sauté pan. Fry the eggs sunny-side up until the edges are browned and the yolks are just set, but still yellow.

Place a cheesy cornbread slab on each of 2 plates. Top each with 2 eggs, some cilantro leaves, and hot sauce to taste. Sprinkle on some extra cheese if you want. Season to taste with salt and pepper. Top with the remaining cornbread slabs.

Doctor it up

Take a tub of your favorite salsa fresca *(or better yet, make your own, see page 88)* and zap it for a minute or two in the microwave. Pour the warm salsa over your sandwich and eat it with a fork.

Serve this

With a heated-up can of red beans, in the winter. A Mexican breakfast on a snowy morning is nothing but pure harmony.

What to drink

My friend Tim won't even *consider* eating this without a shot of Herradura tequila. Actually, he won't consider doing much of anything without a shot of Herradura, but that's a story for another time.

makes two 9-by-5-inch loaves

maple–banana bread coffee cake

Say, "I made banana bread" and people go, "Oh, yum. I *looove* banana bread." Say, "I made coffee cake" and people go, "No way! I *looove* coffee cake!" Say them both together and you'll wish you were wearing a raincoat. For this crumby-bready concoction *(which was a perfectly good banana bread recipe from* The Joy of Cooking *until I got my hands on it)*, you need really ripe bananas. I'm talking black on the outside and totally mushy. If your bananas are firm or yellow at all, put them aside and wait a week. Otherwise, your cake will suck. Also, when I say room temperature for your eggs and butter, I mean it. If they're too cold, they won't incorporate correctly.

Nonstick **cooking spray**, such as Pam, for greasing the pans

FOR THE **TOPPING**

1 cup crushed-up **graham crackers**

1 cup **pecans** or **walnuts**, chopped

½ cup firmly packed **light brown sugar**

¼ cup pure **maple syrup**

4 tablespoons *(½ stick)* **unsalted butter**, melted *(throw it in a coffee cup, then zap it in the microwave for 30 to 40 seconds)*

FOR THE **CAKE**

6 tablespoons *(¾ stick)* **unsalted butter**, at room temperature

½ cup firmly packed **light brown sugar**

¼ cup pure **maple syrup**

1 teaspoon **vanilla extract**

1½ cups **all-purpose flour**

½ teaspoon **salt**

½ teaspoon **baking soda**

½ teaspoon **baking powder**

2 large **eggs**, at room temperature

4 big **bananas**, very ripe, peeled and smashed into a paste

¾ cup **pecans** or **walnuts**, finely chopped

continued

Put the rack in the lower third of the oven and preheat to 350°F. Spray two 9-by-5-inch loaf pans with the cooking spray.

make the topping

Put all the topping ingredients into a food processor. Pulse until crumbly and moist. No processor? Find your wisk. Set aside.

make the cake

In a large bowl, beat together the butter, brown sugar, maple syrup, and vanilla until creamy, about 2 minutes with a mixer on high speed or about 5 minutes by hand.

In another bowl, whisk together the flour, salt, baking soda, and baking powder. Beat into the butter mixture until blended together. Add the eggs and beat until smooth. Fold in the bananas and nuts, distributing evenly.

Divide the batter between the prepared pans. Bang your pans on the counter to settle the batter to the bottom. Top each pan with half of the topping, dragging a knife in a squiggle through the batter to just barely incorporate a little bit of the topping down into the batter. Bang your pans again.

Bake until a toothpick or bamboo skewer stuck into the middle of each loaf comes out mostly clean. *(Some crumbs are OK, but no raw batter.)* They should take about 1 hour. Let cool for 5 minutes in the pans, then turn out onto wire racks. Slice like bread and serve hot. Toast the leftovers.

Doctor it up

Get your fiber on and add a handful of raisins or dried apricots that you've coarsely chopped to the cake batter.

Serve this

With plenty of room-temperature cream cheese.

What to drink

Duh. It's called coffee cake, chief.

blueberry pancakes

If you're looking for someone to tell you that you absolutely _must_ make your own pancake mix because it's either *(a)* better or *(b)* cheaper or *(c)* easier or *(d)* more virtuous, keep looking. I've never had anything bad to say about Bisquick. It's cheap and it works and there's no shame in it. But who the hell wants to pull on shoes—not to mention pants—and haul over to the supermarket on Sunday morning when you discover you've run out? By the way, if you want to double the recipe, I'm all for it.

1 pint **fresh blueberries** or
    2 cups thawed and drained
    frozen blueberries

2 tablespoons **sugar**

    A few gratings of **nutmeg**

FOR THE PANCAKES

2 cups **all-purpose flour**

1 tablespoon **baking powder**

2 tablespoons **sugar**

1 teaspoon **salt**

2 large **eggs**, lightly beaten

1 cup **buttermilk**, plus a
    tablespoon or two more if you
    need it

4 tablespoons *(½ stick)* **unsalted
    butter**, melted, plus more for
    serving

    Pure **maple syrup**, warmed in
    a Pyrex pitcher in the microwave
    until just hot, for serving

continued

In a small bowl, combine the blueberries, sugar, and nutmeg. Set aside.

make the pancakes

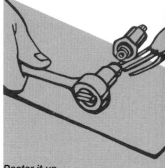

Combine the flour, baking powder, sugar, and salt in a large bowl. No need to sift it, just use a whisk. Whisk in the eggs until combined. Whisk in the buttermilk and melted butter. Don't worry about making the batter perfectly smooth, and for sure don't overwork it, or your pancakes will get all tough.

Heat up your pan. If you've got a great old cast-iron frying pan that's well-seasoned, use it. If not, melt just a little bit of butter in a sauté pan, using just enough to barely cover the bottom. Using a ¼-cup measuring cup or other scooping device, scoop a few tablespoons of batter into the pan. (Personally, I like a lot of small ones, rather than just a couple huge ones.) Spoon several berries over the pancake before it sets. When bubbles cover the top of your pancake, flip it and cook just until the bottom is golden brown. *(Warning: It is a well-documented fact of science that the first pancake never works. Ever. Give it the bird and toss it into the garbage. The second one will be perfect.)* Repeat to make the remaining pancakes, keeping the finished cakes warm on a platter in a low *(200°F)* oven.

Serve with the butter and maple syrup.

Doctor it up

You can make pancakes with pretty much anything you want. I love blueberries, but if you're into bananas or chopped and toasted pecans, have at it.

Serve this

With plenty of bacon that you've broiled and drained on paper towels to crisp up. *(Note: Always make extra bacon so you have some for sandwiches at lunchtime.)*

What to drink

Freshly squeezed orange juice, one of life's greatest pleasures.

hash 'n' eggs

Picture it. The party's over, you've had a couple, it's late, and you're home. Alone. Forecast is for passing out in your socks and sleeping in late. Why not knock breakfast out of the way now, while you're still up?

2	tablespoons **unsalted butter**, plus 1 teaspoon
1	tablespoons **olive oil**
2	large **russet potatoes**, diced very small *(about ¼-inch cubes)* *(Don't bother peeling them unless you really want to.)*
½	pound **ground turkey** or **chicken**
1	medium **yellow onion**, diced
1	medium **zucchini**, diced
	Salt and **pepper**
½	cup **chicken stock** *(page 108)*, canned broth, or water, or more as needed
2	large **eggs**

continued

In a large sauté pan, melt the 2 tablespoons butter with the olive oil until hot. Sauté the potatoes and turkey until golden, about 10 minutes. Add the onion, zucchini, and salt and pepper and sauté until the zucchini begins to brown, about 3 to 4 minutes.

Add the chicken stock to pan, scraping up any browned bits from the bottom of the pan and incorporating them into the liquid. Bring to a boil, then lower the heat to a simmer. Allow the stock to evaporate completely, about 10 minutes. Test the potatoes for doneness: When the potatoes are soft, but not mushy, and totally brown on the bottom, they're done. If necessary, add and cook off another ¼ to ½ cup of stock or water.

Scrape the hash onto a plate, making sure to scrape up all the browned pieces stuck to the bottom of the pan. Fry the eggs in the 1 teaspoon butter, sunny-side up. Think runny yolk and crispy brown edges. Slide the eggs onto the hash and immediately cut them into it so your yolks run all through it.

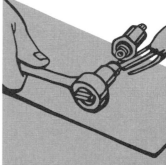

Doctor it up

Tabasco sauce was invented for this. So was *(believe it or not, but try it)* mayonnaise.

Serve this

When your game didn't work.

What to drink

Resist the urge for a nightcap and have water. Or don't, and enjoy one last glass of sipping tequila. Just don't blame me tomorrow.

I love oatmeal. I have it for breakfast almost every morning. But whoever invented instant oatmeal has no place at my table. That stuff is nothing but trouble, a pasty, gummy, oat-flavored slop that gets stuck in your teeth for the rest of the day, doing nothing for your social life. *(Well, at least that's what happened to me.)* Maybe they go for that kind of thing in *your* world, Mr. Instant-Oatmeal-Inventor, but not in mine. It's all about old-fashioned oats for me, which taste about a million times better, but take only a couple of minutes longer. Some people say you should salt your oats while you're cooking, but Alton Brown says not to, and he's right, so I just add a little salt at the end.

2   cups **milk** *(I like to keep it whole, but if you want, use 2 percent. Don't use skim, however, because it will suck.)*

1½ cups old-fashioned **rolled oats**

2   tablespoons pure **maple syrup**

Any or all of the following **add-ins,** your call:

½   cup chopped **walnuts, pecans,** or **almonds**

A handful of **raisins**

All-fruit **Popsicle** *(melts into a fabulous fruit syrup)*

Crumbled **bacon**

A handful of **cereal**

A couple of gratings of **nutmeg**

A few **berries,** frozen or fresh

2   tablespoons of your favorite **jam** *(apricot, strawberry, whatever)*

1   teaspoon ground **cinnamon**

Milk, cream, or **half-and-half**

Brown sugar

Unsalted butter and **salt** for serving

oats

In a saucepan over medium-high heat, bring the milk to a very low boil. Don't let it rip, or it'll be all over your stove. Stir in the oats and maple syrup and bring it back to a low boil. Drop the heat to medium and continue to cook for 5 more minutes, stirring a few times.

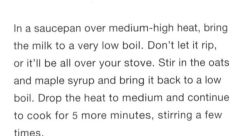

Remove from the heat and stir in your add-ins. Dish it up and serve with a big pat of butter and a sprinkle of salt.

Doctor it up

Scoop this into an ovenproof dish, then sprinkle raw or brown sugar over the top. Slide it under the broiler for a couple of minutes, and voilà: oatmeal brûlée.

Serve this

Weekdays.

What to drink

Your first cup of coffee for the day.

overnight baked french toast wit

serves 4

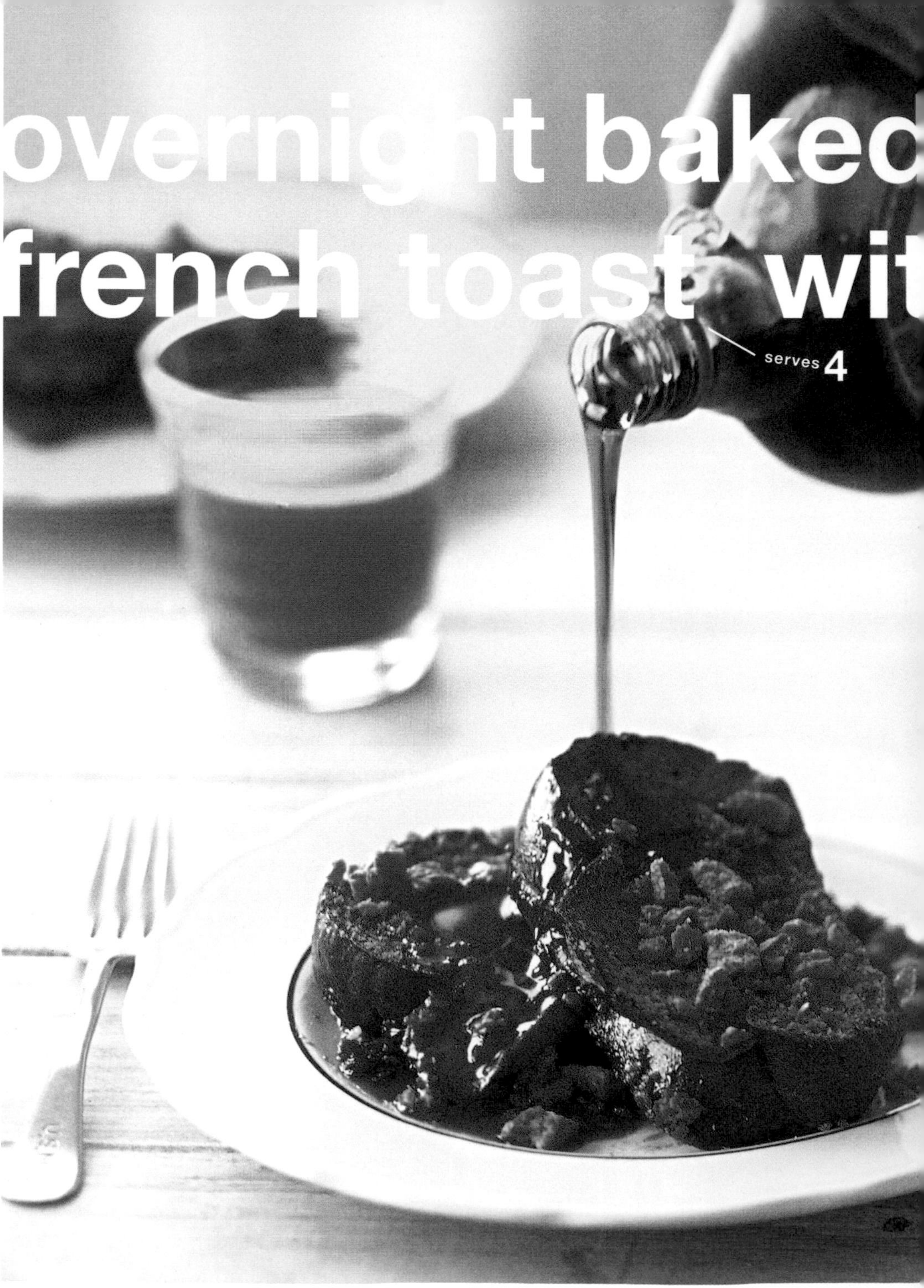

cap'n crumble

French toast is the known world's most effective SDS *(Syrup Delivery System)*, and yet, even *that* distinction shortchanges it. This baked French toast is warm, soft, sweet, and satisfying, guaranteed to send you back into bed for a long, slow post-breakfast . . . nap.

1   cup firmly packed **brown sugar**

4   tablespoons *(½ stick)* **unsalted butter**, melted

3   **eggs**

1   cup **milk**

2   teaspoons **vanilla extract**

1   teaspoon **ground cinnamon**

1   loaf day-old **French, challah,** or **country bread**, cut into slices about 1½ inches thick *(Up to 3 days old, just slightly stale. Don't use anything moldy.)*

     A few gratings of **nutmeg**

2   cups **Cap'n Crunch**

     Pure **maple syrup**, warmed in a Pyrex pitcher in the microwave until just hot, for serving

continued

Sprinkle the brown sugar over the bottom of a 9-by-13-inch baking dish, covering the dish evenly. Drizzle the melted butter all over the top.

Mix together the eggs, milk, vanilla, and cinnamon in a large bowl. Dip a piece of bread into the mixture to coat on both sides *(don't drown them)*, then place in baking dish. Repeat with each slice of bread. When the dish is full, grate some nutmeg over the top. Cover and refrigerate overnight.

Next morning, remove the French toast from the fridge when you get up. Allow it to come to room temperature while you preheat the oven to 350°F. Bake, uncovered, for 30 minutes. Crumble the Cap'n Crunch over the top and continue to bake for 10 minutes more. Serve hot with the maple syrup.

Doctor it up

Put a scoop of ice cream on this and call it dessert. Hey, it's all semantics.

Serve this

To your overnight guest. Or guests, if you're really lucky.

What to drink

Who says you can't pop a bottle of bubbly on any given Saturday?

Gentlemen, Start Your Ovens

fried country ham and grits with maple syrup

Grits come in all shapes and textures, from firm and tightly packed to soft, loose, and creamy. If you're trying to impress someone who's easily impressed, make grits for dinner and call them *polenta*. It's the same damn thing. As for the ham steaks, buy the ones that look like the cartoon ham steaks you see in old Road Runner cartoons. At the grocery store, you'll find them in the meat section, near the pork chops. Don't use the ham in the deli section or over by the cheese. And remember, they're already fully cooked and smoked, so all you're really doing is heating them up.

2   cups **water**

3   tablespoons **unsalted butter**

A few drops of **olive oil**

1 or 2 **country ham steaks**

½   cup **grits** *(Quaker Quick Grits are good)*

Salt

½   cup pure **maple syrup**, or to taste *(Use the real stuff here. Mrs. Butterworth has her appeal, but let's not be so cheap.)*

½   cup **shredded cheese** *(such as Cheddar, Jack, or mozzarella, or crumbled goat cheese or, if you like the blues, Roquefort)*

Put your water in a medium saucepan, covered, over high heat to boil.

Melt 1 tablespoon of the butter in a large sauté pan over medium-high heat. Add a drop or two of olive oil to keep your butter from burning. When it starts to bubble, lay the ham steak(s) in the pan. Resist the urge to start moving the steak around. Leave it alone and let it sizzle for 4 minutes.

Meanwhile, your water is boiling, so stir in your grits. Stir carefully until the water comes back to a boil and the grits stop foaming, about 1 to 2 minutes, removing them from the heat momentarily if needed to keep them from foaming over.

continued

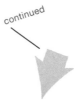

When the foaming subsides, gently stir in 2 big pinches of salt and 1 tablespoon butter. Turn the heat down to medium-low and simmer until they're tender, about 5 to 7 minutes, stirring gently every 2 minutes.

While the grits are simmering, check your ham steak. It should be nicely browned on the bottom. Adjust the heat if necessary, flip, and cook 3 to 4 more minutes.

Meanwhile, warm the maple syrup in the microwave using a Pyrex pitcher, about 1 minute on high for ½ cup, or until hot to the touch. Stir in the remaining 1 tablespoon butter. *(Make more syrup if you want, adding a tablespoon of butter for each ½ cup of syrup.)* Set aside to cool.

Stir the cheese into the grits. Taste and add more salt if they need it. *(Don't salt before you add the cheese, or your grits will be too salty.)*

Serve hot, laying the ham steak over the grits and pouring the buttered maple syrup over all.

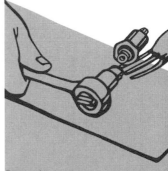

Doctor it up

With an egg or two, fried over-easy.

Serve this

On moving day. This stuff sticks to your ribs.

What to drink

Your second Coke of the morning, like any self-respecting redneck.

C02 All-Day Breakfast

serves **2**

re-fried donuts

with cream cheese dip

Don't ever let anyone tell you to throw away those week-old Entenmann's cake donuts. There's gold in them thar donuts. And don't let anyone tell you this dish is junk food, either. There's real orange juice in that dip.

FOR THE **DONUTS**

4   **cake donuts**, nice and firm, preferably a day or two old

2   **eggs**

½   cup **milk**

1   tablespoon **unsalted butter**, or more as needed

FOR THE **CREAM CHEESE DIP**

1   box *(1 pound)* **powdered sugar**

A few gratings of **nutmeg**

2   tablespoons **cream cheese**

Zest of 1 **juice orange**

4 to 6 tablespoons **fresh orange juice** *(use the same orange you just zested)*, or more as needed for the fried donuts

continued

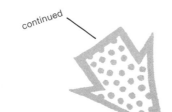

make the dip

Mix together all the dip ingredients in a large Pyrex pitcher or microwave-safe bowl. Introduce it to your microwave for 30 seconds on high, then remove and stir vigorously. Add more orange juice if necessary to reach the desired dipping consistency. Set aside.

make the donuts

Slice the donuts in half through the middle, like you would slice a bagel. Beat the eggs with the milk in a shallow dish. Dip the donut slices into the egg mixture, coating completely.

In a large sauté pan over high heat, melt the butter until it foams. Fry the coated donut slices in batches *(don't crowd the pan)*, flat-side down, until browned on the bottom. Flip. Continue cooking until browned on both sides. Add a little more butter if needed. Serve hot with the cream cheese dip.

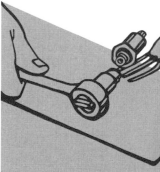

Doctor it up

Don't like orange? Use lemon juice and zest. Or use milk. Or rum.

Serve this

When you've got plenty of toothpaste in the house. This stuff will make your teeth rattle.

What to drink

Got milk?

susan o's
"last resort"

cures 1 hangover

My friend Susan is sometimes a rock star, sometimes an artist, sometimes a sex goddess, and always a really smart lady who drips attitude and style. She also has some of the most impressive cleavage I've ever seen, and if you're ever stuck with a hangover *(and who isn't every now and then?)*, then Susan is the woman to see. This is a variation on the traditional prairie oyster.

1   fresh, raw, unbeaten **egg**

1   shake of **Worcestershire sauce**

1   shake of **Tabasco sauce**

2   tablespoons premium **bourbon**

    A pinch of **red pepper flakes**

Combine all the ingredients in a small glass. Do not stir the mixture. Shoot it in one gulp, then head back to bed until your hangover recedes. Do not answer the phone.

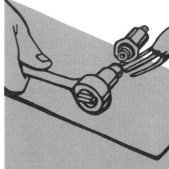

Doctor it up
Feel like adding a tequila floater? That makes you the biggest man there is.

Serve this
With coffee, cigarettes, and lies about what went on last night.

What to drink
A big glass of water, room temperature.

C02   All-Day Breakfast

hey dj! make me a sandwich!

Making a great sandwich is like being a great DJ. A great DJ scours the record shops, finds the best songs, then puts together a set that tells a story. But if the songs suck, not even the best DJ can make a set that works. *(Just ask any wedding DJ who's been asked to put "Mony Mony" in the mix.)* For a DJ, it all starts with the songs.

It's the same deal when you're making a sandwich: It all starts with the ingredients. You have to scour the grocery store for the best ingredients, then put them together in a way that tells a story. And if any one of your ingredients sucks, your whole sandwich will, too.

And by the way, sandwiches shouldn't just be eaten for lunch. Sandwiches can be breakfast, lunch, dinner, and snack food. And not only that, they can be some pretty damn fine and elegant eats, too. There is no time or place on the planet when a sandwich isn't welcome.

viches

crab salad sandwiches on hot dog rolls

serves 2

It's all about the butter in this recipe, from the buttery dressing for the crab salad to the buttered, fried hot dog rolls. So don't skimp, even if whoever you're making these for is on some crappy trend diet. Just tell them it's low-carb. Or low-cal. Or whatever the diet du jour dictates.

Unsalted butter for the rolls, plus 4 tablespoons *(½ stick)* melted and cooled

2   **hot dog rolls**

8   ounces **lump crabmeat** *(pick it over to get rid of any renegade shell pieces that might be hiding)*

2   tablespoons **mayonnaise**

2   stalks **celery**, finely chopped

½   **red bell pepper**, finely chopped

1   teaspoon **celery seed**

2   tablespoons **dried minced onion**

Lawry's seasoned salt

Freshly ground **black pepper**

1   **tomato**, sliced

continued

Heat up a large sauté pan. Butter the hot dog rolls liberally and fry, butter-side down, until golden brown. Remove from the heat, flip the rolls, and cover to keep warm in the pan.

In a small bowl, use a fork to mix the crabmeat, melted butter, mayo, celery, bell pepper, celery seed, minced onion, and seasoned salt and pepper to taste.

Line the warm hot dog rolls with tomato slices, then spoon the crab salad over the top.

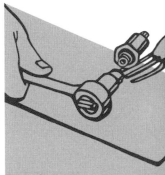

Doctor it up

Dig out that mandoline that Mom gave you last Christmas and shave some Brussels sprouts into the crab mixture. *(No mandoline? Me either. Forget it.)*

Serve this

With a big ol' bag of potato chips.

What to drink

Get girly and try a crisp, cold rosé. If you hate it, curse me and grab a beer.

skirt steak sandwiches on garlic bread

Some people like flank steak or sirloin for their sandwiches, and I respect that. Me, I prefer a skirt steak, which has all kinds of flavor, and a more tender bite, than flank. Don't make this without opening the windows, or the steak will smoke you out of your kitchen faster than Cheech and/or Chong.

FOR THE GARLIC BREAD

2 **garlic cloves**, smashed and minced

4 tablespoons *(½ stick)* **unsalted butter**, at room temperature

¼ cup *(ish)* fresh **parsley leaves,** finely chopped

Salt

1 loaf fresh or day-old **French** or **Italian bread**

FOR THE STEAK

1 **skirt steak**, about 1½ pounds

Salt and **pepper**

1 tablespoon **unsalted butter**

FOR THE SANDWICHES

Red onion slices

Red leaf lettuce leaves

Beefsteak tomato slices

Salt and **pepper**

C03 Sandwiches

continued

make the garlic bread

Preheat the oven to 350°F. In a small bowl, mix together the garlic, butter, parsley, and salt to taste until well combined. Let sit for at least 15 minutes or up to several hours. *(The longer it sits, the more the flavors will blend together.)* Working lengthwise, halve the loaf of bread like a hero, then in half crosswise to make 4 equal pieces *(they should be about 6 inches long)*. Slather each piece with the garlic butter, reserving about a teaspoon or so for another slather when you serve. Place on a baking sheet, reduce the oven temperature to 300°F, and bake for about 20 minutes.

make the steak

While bread is baking, season the steak with salt and pepper. In a medium sauté pan over high heat, melt the butter until it sizzles. Sear the steak for 2 minutes on one side *(don't move it around)*, then flip and sear for 4 minutes. Then turn back over and cook for 2 more minutes. Remove from the heat and check for doneness. *(Make a small slit in the middle of the steak with a paring knife. It should be just a little too pink since it will continue cooking off the heat.)* Set the steak aside and allow it to rest for a few minutes before slicing.

make the sandwiches

While steak is resting, stack the 2 bottom pieces of the bread with the onion slices, lettuce leaves, and tomatoes. Sprinkle with salt and pepper to taste. Spread the reserved garlic butter on the 2 top pieces of the bread. After the steak has rested for 5 to 10 minutes, slice it thinly against the grain, making small strips. Pile the steak on top of the tomatoes, then top with the bread tops. Press firmly on the sandwich so all the meat juices mingle with the butter and saturate the bread. Eat while still warm.

Doctor it up

Fry yourself a couple of eggs and have this for breakfast.

Serve this

When Dad comes to visit.

What to drink

A good California Zinfandel (ask your vintner for help choosing one).

There are two kinds of people in the world: Them that likes a tuna melt and them that don't. I am in the first camp. Some people say that you can only use Monterey Jack cheese here, but personally I prefer a really sharp Cheddar cheese. It gets browner and crispier, and has a stronger flavor, which is a good backdrop to the creamy tuna. Gross, I just said creamy tuna.

FOR THE **TUNA SALAD**

1 can **chunk white tuna in oil**

2 tablespoons **mayonnaise**

2 teaspoons **dried minced onion**

1 teaspoon **celery seed**

Juice of ½ **lemon**

1 stalk **celery**, finely chopped

Lawry's seasoned salt

Freshly ground **black pepper**

FOR THE **SANDWICHES**

4 slices **bread** (sourdough, country white, or seedless rye)

½ cup shredded **sharp Cheddar cheese**

serves 2

tastes like

make the tuna salad

Combine all the ingredients in a medium bowl. Taste and adjust the salt and pepper accordingly.

make the sandwiches

Preheat the broiler. On a baking sheet, toast the bread slices lightly on one side. Flip the bread over and divide the tuna salad equally on top of the untoasted sides, then sprinkle the cheese over the tops. Return to the broiler until the cheese melts and begins to brown on the edges, about 3 to 4 minutes. *(Watch it closely, 'cause these will burn faster than you can pick that wedgie.)* Serve open-faced.

Doctor it up

B-A-C-O-N. Capers are good, too.

Serve this

After midnight.

What to drink

The last beer of the night.

tuna melt

grilled cheese and onions

The first time you make yourself a grilled cheese sandwich, you should ignore this recipe and simply fry in butter a couple slices of Wonder Bread with an individually wrapped American cheese-like product in between. *(Just remember to unwrap the cheese.)* It'll be delicious. The *second* time you make yourself a grilled cheese sandwich, make this one. Manchego cheese makes a rich, extra-gooey sandwich with plenty of flavor.

FOR THE **CARAMELIZED ONIONS**

1 tablespoon **unsalted butter**

1 tablespoon **olive oil**

1 large **onion**, sliced into thin rings

FOR THE **SANDWICHES**

Unsalted butter

4 slices **white bread**

8 slices **manchego cheese**

A few **roasted peppers** from a jar

Ketchup, at room temperature *(This is important, because ketchup has a much better taste at room temperature. If yours is cold, hit it with the microwave for a few seconds, then stir.)*

sandwiches with peppers

make the **caramelized onions**

In a small sauté pan over medium-high heat, melt the butter with the oil until hot but not smoking. Sauté the onion for 20 to 25 minutes, stirring every now and then, until they're deep brown and smell really good.

make the sandwiches

Heat up a large frying pan over high heat. Butter both sides of the bread slices. Build 2 sandwiches with the cheese, a forkful of caramelized onions, and a few roasted peppers. When the pan is hot, lift the sandwiches into pan. Fry for 3 minutes per side, or until the bread is toasty brown and the cheese is melted. And careful when you flip it, or you'll be wearing it.

Cut the sandwiches in half and serve, with the ketchup for dipping.

Doctor it up

Not to beat a dead horse, but how about some bacon?

Serve this

With the tomato soup on page 105 after another day of bullshit at work.

What to drink

Coke. And if you like a little Jack in your Coke, so be it.

C03 Sandwiches

pressed salumi
with roasted ga

When it comes to food, Italy has everyone beat. Their ingredients, especially olives and olive oil, cured meats, and certain cheeses, are the best on the planet. So, do this: Ditch the supermarket and sniff out the best local Italian deli with the best imported ingredients in your neighborhood *(this may take a few tries, and your allegiances may shift over time, but it's worth doing),* and buy everything for your pressed sandwiches there.

2 **garlic heads**

Olive oil for drizzling

1 large loaf **Italian bread** *(day-old is best, but fresh will work)*

Balsamic vinegar for drizzling

8 slices thinly sliced **prosciutto**

8 slices **soppressata**

8 slices **mortadella**

8 shavings **Parmesan cheese**, preferably Parmigiano-Reggiano

1 ball fresh **mozzarella**, sliced

1 small jar **roasted peppers**

1 small jar **marinated artichokes**

2 tablespoons **salt-packed capers**, quickly rinsed

1 bunch **fresh basil**

Preheat the oven to 400°F. Slice the garlic heads in half across the equator. Drizzle with olive oil, wrap in aluminum foil, and roast for 35 minutes. Let cool for 15 minutes, then unwrap and squeeze out the soft pulp.

sandwich

rlic

Slice the loaf of bread in half lengthwise. Lay on top of a sheet of heavy-duty aluminum foil. Spread the roasted garlic onto one cut side of the bread. Drizzle both cut sides of the bread liberally with olive oil and balsamic vinegar. Layer the meats, cheeses, vegetables, capers, and basil on top of bottom bread slice. Drizzle with oil and vinegar again. Cap the sandwich, then wrap the foil tightly around it *(you might need to double-wrap it)* and place it on a baking sheet. Press down on the sandwich with your heaviest frying pan. Use a brick or another pot for weight to complete the press for the sandwich. Ideally, you press it in the fridge overnight, turning it over halfway through, but if you can't wait until tomorrow, press at room temperature for at least 2 hours, flipping it after 1 hour.

Without unwrapping, slice the sandwich into 4 equal servings.

Doctor it up

Have your way with it, doc. Change out the cheese, sub in a different meat, throw on more vegetables. Just keep it well oiled.

Serve this

On a hike.

What to drink

An inexpensive Chianti.

meatball

These go down perfect on Sunday nights, when you've got some serious television watching to catch up on. Produce these babies *(they're cake to make)* and you're the only hero in the kitchen.

2 fresh **hero rolls**, split

½ cup **tomato sauce** *(page 144, or use your favorite jarred sauce)*

8 medium-sized **meatballs** *(page 125)*

½ cup shredded **mozzarella cheese**

¼ cup grated **Parmesan cheese**, preferably Parmigiano-Reggiano

1 **garlic clove**, halved

heroes

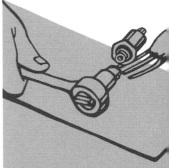

Preheat the oven to 375°F. Lay the roll halves, cut-side up, on a baking sheet. Spread half of the tomato sauce on each bottom piece. Place 4 meatballs on the second piece of each hero. Bake for 10 minutes, to warm the meatballs and sauce and toast the tops of the rolls.

Remove from the oven. Sprinkle the cheeses over the meatballs and rub the hero tops with garlic. Return to the oven and toast for another 5 minutes, or until the cheese is melted and bubbly. If desired, slide under the broiler for extra-browned cheese.

Doctor it up

Add roasted peppers, sautéed onions, cooked spinach, roasted garlic cloves, a couple of anchovies, whatever. Check the fridge, there's always something in there.

Serve this

On Monday night, using Sunday's meatballs.

What to drink

The last, unfinished dribble of last night's red wine. *(Yeah, right.)*

ho chi
minh hero

I first discovered Banh Mi sandwiches, a mishmash of French Colonial and local Vietnamese flavors, at a little Vietnamese sandwich counter in New York's Chinatown. You can cheat the fillings on this sandwich, but don't cheat the bread, and don't cheat the butter.

2 teaspoons **unsalted butter,** at room temperature

2 teaspoons **mayonnaise**

One 8-inch fresh **French baguette,** sliced in half lengthwise *(find the best bread maker in your town and buy their freshest loaf)*

3 to 4 ounces *pâté de campagne* or chicken liver pâté, at room temperature *(find this in the fancy cheese section)*

4 to 6 slices good-quality **deli ham**

1 small **crunchy sweet pickle,** cut into strips

1 handful bagged **cole slaw mix** *(cabbage and carrot shavings)*

1 small **jalapeño,** sliced *(The white ribs and the seeds are the hottest parts of the jalapeño. The more of that stuff that makes it into your sandwich, the hotter it'll be.)*

½ bunch **fresh cilantro sprigs**

A few **fresh mint leaves** *(check the backyard)*

Hot sauce or chile paste, your choice

Spread the butter and mayonnaise on the cut sides of the bread. Slather the pâté on both sides. Layer on the ham, vegetables, herbs, and hot sauce. Chow.

Doctor it up

Skip the pâté and use chicken meat torn from a precooked chicken.

Serve this

When the bread at the store looks really good.

What to drink

Very, very cold beer. Or very, very cold Coca-Cola.

serves **4**

**all-day
sandwi**

If you have a barbecue pit in your backyard, ignore this recipe, because you can definitely make a better pulled-pork sandwich than I can. But for the rest of us pitless losers, this oven-cured pork shoulder totally delivers. You can make this with a store-bought spice rub *(there are some pretty good ones out there)*, but making your own makes you a better man. Ditto with the barbecue sauce. Warning: This recipe takes all day. Actually, it also takes some work the night before. But it's way worth it.

FOR THE **SPICE RUB**

1 tablespoon **celery seed**

2 tablespoons **dark brown sugar**

¼ cup **paprika**

2 teaspoons **ground cumin**

2 teaspoons **dry mustard**

1 teaspoon **garlic powder**

1 tablespoon **dried sage leaves**

1 tablespoon **red pepper flakes**, finely crushed

2 teaspoons **salt**

FOR THE **PORK**

1 **bone-in pork shoulder**, about 6 pounds

2 slices **bacon**, snipped with scissors into small pieces

2 teaspoons **olive oil**

1 medium **onion**, diced

1 **carrot**, peeled and diced

2 **bay leaves**

½ can *(6 ounces)* **beer**

pulled-pork
ches

continued

FOR THE **SAUCE**

¼ to ½ cup **water**

Reserved **spice rub** *(page 67)*

¼ cup **ketchup**

½ cup **red wine vinegar**

¼ cup **soy sauce**

Juice of 1 **orange**

Any accumulated **pan juices**
from the plate holding the pork

FOR THE **SANDWICHES**

8 slices soft **white country bread**,
or 4 seeded rolls

1 medium **red onion**, thinly sliced

make the spice rub

Whisk together all the ingredients in a bowl.
*(If you have a mortar and pestle, crush them
all together.)*

make the pork

Massage three-fourths of the spice rub mixture
into the pork shoulder, being sure to cover shoulder completely. Get all up in it and leave no cor-
ner or cranny unrubbed. Save the rest of the rub
for the barbecue sauce. Cover the meat with
plastic wrap and refrigerate overnight.

First thing the next morning, preheat the oven to 300°F. On the stove top, in a large Dutch oven over high heat, sauté the bacon in the olive oil until the fat has rendered. Sear the pork shoulder on all sides, browning well, about 2 minutes per side. Add the onion, carrot, bay leaves, and beer. Cover the pot and transfer to the oven. Bake for about 4 hours, or until the meat pulls easily from the bone. Transfer to a plate and let sit until ready to shred. *(If you don't have a Dutch oven, sear the pork in a large frying pan, then transfer to a covered roasting dish to bake.)*

make the sauce

Blot the excess fat from the Dutch oven using a paper towel. Place on the stove top over high heat, add the ¼ cup water, and scrape up any browned bits from the bottom of the pan. Let these juices bubble and reduce by half, adding more water if necessary, then add the other sauce ingredients. Mix together, adjusting the amounts of the ingredients, to suit your no-doubt picky-ass taste buds.

Use a fork to shred the meat from the pork shoulder. Mix with the sauce.

make the sandwiches

Build the sandwiches on the country bread with the saucy pork and onion slices and serve.

Doctor it up

Lose the bread and just eat this pork with a warmed-up can of beans or a tray of shoestring oven fries. You can screw with the spice rub and sauce recipes all you want. Use cayenne pepper or chile powder in the rub or grated lime peel in the sauce. When you find the best mix for the rub, make extra and keep in the cabinet for next time. It'll still be pretty good for about 6 weeks.

Serve this

At the height of summer, with lots of potato chips.

What to drink

Beer from a can *(preferably the same brand of beer that you used in the pork).*

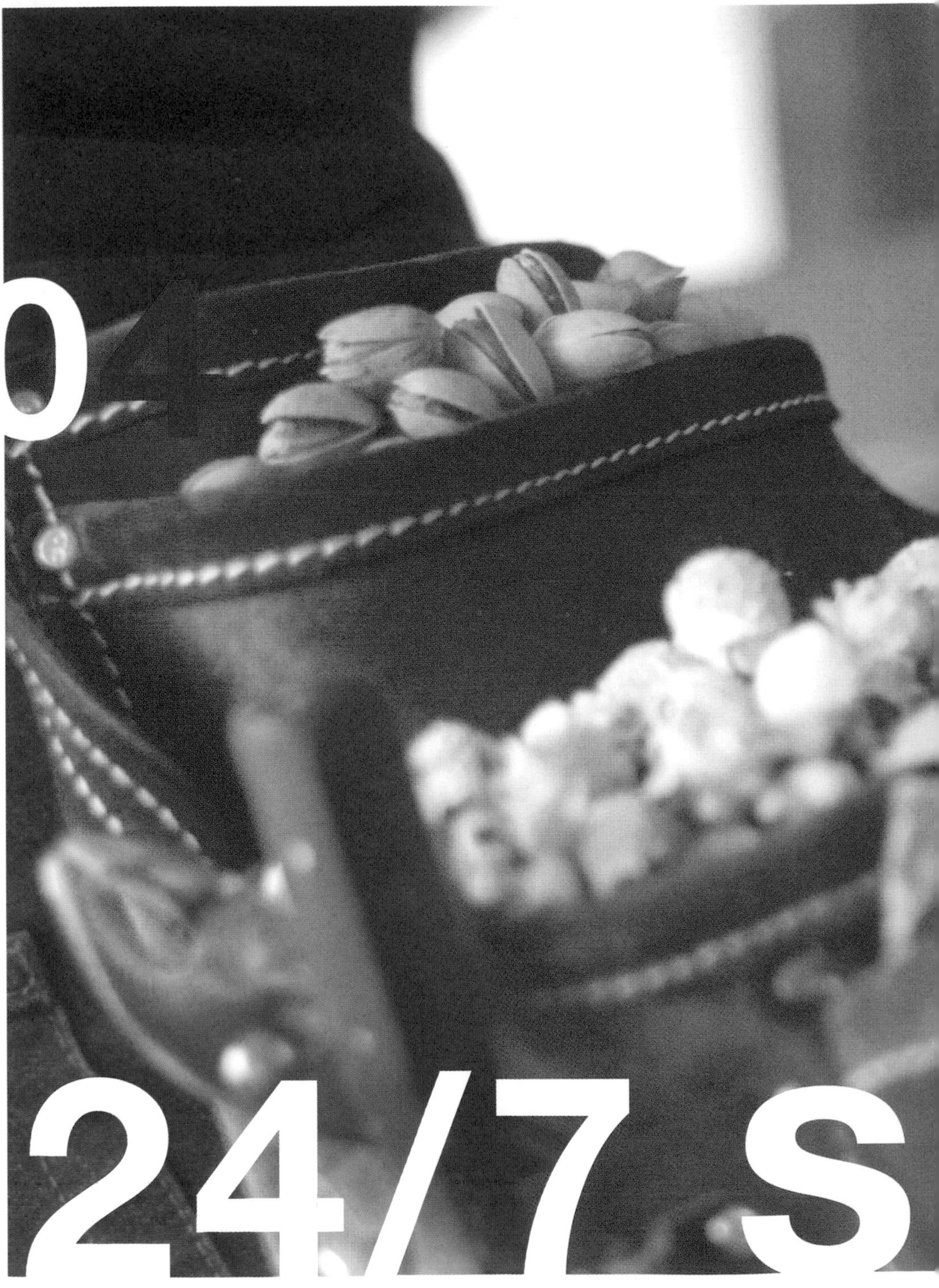

04

24/7 S

it's always snack time!

Let's be completely honest: Many of the world's best snacks, including Doritos, Ring-Dings, and salted peanuts in the shell, have no place in this cookbook, or any cookbook for that matter. They're already perfect.

And I'm about as skeptical as they come when cookbooks tell me to make my own rippled potato chips or Hostess Sno-Balls at home. I suppose it *could* be done, but it probably shouldn't.

But while the world is replete with ample *(and good)* prepackaged snack options, I believe *(and I believe you will, too)* that, there's always room for a little sumpin' sumpin' from your kitchen. Something just as good, just as addictive, as Crunchy Cheetos, only something you throw together yourself.

While most of the snacks here are best enjoyed in front of the television, many of them will travel just as well, so your next nosh is as close as your cargo pockets.

nacks

dip trip

Makes **4** dips; each serves **2** to **4** people

I don't know who paid off the FDA to keep them from making dip its own food group. Enjoy several servings per week, with chips, pretzels, cut-up vegetables, or the onion rings on page 77. Or, a spoon.

FOR THE **DIP BASE**

Two 8-ounce packages **cream cheese**, at room temperature

1 cup **mayonnaise** *(if you hate mayonnaise, use ¾ cup sour cream plus a drizzle of olive oil)*

FOR THE **ROASTED GARLIC DIP**

1 **garlic head**, roasted *(see page 60)*

A few sprigs of **fresh parsley**, stems and leaves, chopped *(experiment with other herbs, like rosemary, sage, or cilantro)*

A drizzling of **olive oil**

Salt and **pepper**

FOR THE **ONION DIP**

1 **onion**, sliced and sautéed until soft and caramelized in 1 teaspoon butter, then cooled

2 tablespoons **dried minced onions**

3 **green onions**, chopped

1 tablespoon **Dijon mustard**

Salt and **pepper**

FOR THE **CLAM DIP**

1 to 2 cans *(10 ounces each)* **minced clams** *(depending on how clammy you like your dip)*

2 tablespoons minced **fresh chives**

2 to 3 strips crisp cooked **bacon**, crumbled

A few gratings of **lemon** zest

Salt and **pepper**

FOR THE **SPICY CHEDDAR DIP**

1 teaspoon **red pepper flakes**

2 tablespoons **ketchup**

¾ cup shredded **Cheddar cheese**

continued

make the dip base

Put the ingredients for the base in a food processor. Pulse several times until well mixed.

make the roasted garlic dip

Remove three-fourths of the dip base from processor and set aside. Add the ingredients for the roasted garlic dip to the processor and pulse until combined, then transfer to a bowl and refrigerate.

make the onion dip

Don't wash the processor yet, just return another one-fourth of the dip base, add the ingredients for the onion dip, and pulse away. Remove, refrigerate. Next!

make the clam dip

For the clam dip, return another one-fourth of the dip base, add the ingredients for the clam dip, and pulse away. Remove, refrigerate. Give the processor a quick wipe.

make the spicy cheddar dip

For the spicy Cheddar dip, return another one-fourth of the dip base, add the ingredients, and pulse away. Remove, refrigerate. *(Do this one last so the other dips don't pick up the heat.)*

Doctor it up

Jalapeños? Ham and pineapple? Sage and feta? Cajun shrimp? Walnut and black olive? Feta and tomato? Wild mushroom? Sour cream and chive? Spinach and artichoke? Somebody stop me.

Serve this

On game day. *(Keeping in mind that with 750 channels on cable, it's always game day.)*

What to drink

Nothing complements a nice gooey dip like a nice cold Coke.

chile con queso (y cojones)

Chile con queso *(or "CCQ" to those of us who've waited tables)* is Spanish,
I think, for "a whole lot of love." Think of it as a bowl of cheese, and think of your
tortilla chips as edible spoons. I've seen people skip the chips altogether and
just drink it with a straw. OK, I'm lying, but it *is* that good. Remember, the more
chiles you add, the more manly you are.

1   small can *(about 6 ounces)* **green
chile sauce**

1   small can *(about 6 ounces)*
chopped jalapeños *(if you can't
stand the heat, use less)*

1   can *(about 10 ½ ounces)* **cream of
celery soup**

1   small can *(about 10 ounces)*
chopped tomatoes

1   pound **shredded cheese** *(find a
bag of preshredded Mexican Blend
or shred your own block of Jack
or Cheddar)*

   Tortilla chips for serving *(Use
   your favorite chip. My favorite chip
   is the round white restaurant
   kind, but you can use Cool Ranch
   if you must.)*

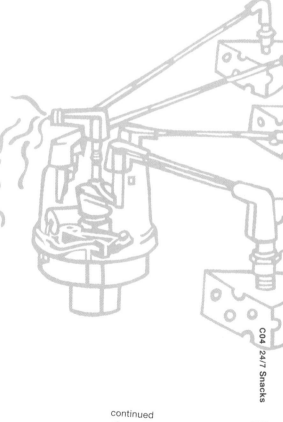

continued

Warm the chile sauce, jalapeños, and celery soup in a medium saucepan over medium-high heat. Keep your eye on it and stir slowly. The idea is to keep things moving so nothing burns. Leave it alone and the stuff at the bottom of the pot will burn, and that would suck.

Strain the tomatoes and discard the liquid. Add to the chile mixture, stirring gently. When the mixture starts to bubble *(before it's a full-on boil)*, remove from heat. Add a handful of cheese, stirring constantly. Continue adding cheese and stirring until smooth. Hit it with another small blast of low to medium heat if necessary.

Serve with tortilla chips. Or straws.

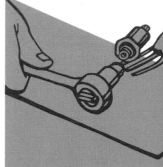

Doctor it up

Use different smoked chiles or different cheese mixtures. Or better yet, toss on a floater shot of your favorite tequila.

Serve this

For landmark television events like Election Night. Or any *Baywatch* reunion.

What to drink

A sturdy Mexican beer. Negra Modelo works for me.

Gentlemen, Start Your Ovens

76

beer-battered onion rings

Unlike French fries, onion rings are easy to make, and make good, at home. These are baked, not fried, which means they won't splatter oil all over your kitchen, and your jeans will still fit. Who's your fry daddy now?

1 cup **all-purpose flour**

1 teaspoon **Lawry's seasoned salt**

2 teaspoons **paprika**

½ teaspoon **garlic powder**

Freshly ground **black pepper**

1 **egg**

½ can *(6 ounces)* **beer**

2 cups **Corn Chex**, crushed into a powder

3 large **yellow onions**, sliced into ½-inch rings

Preheat the oven to 375°F. Line a baking sheet with aluminum foil, shiny-side up. In a medium bowl, whisk together the flour, seasoned salt, paprika, garlic powder, and pepper to taste. Turn out onto a plate. In a small bowl, beat together the egg and beer. Set aside. Turn the crushed Corn Chex out onto another plate.

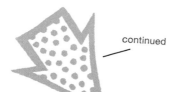

continued

Working with one onion ring at a time, dip a ring into the seasoned flour, tap off the excess, dip into the egg mixture, and finally, dip into the crushed Corn Chex. Lay the onion rings in a single layer on the prepared baking sheet. Mix together the remaining egg mixture and Corn Chex and pour over the onion rings. Bake for about 20 minutes, until golden brown. Serve hot.

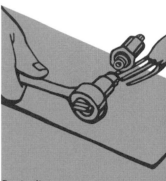

Doctor it up

Use this batter for shrimp, fish fillets, vegetables . . . whatever you want to fry/bake.

Serve this

With dip. Need dip? See pages 73–74.

What to drink

You already cracked a beer and used half, which means there are five and a half left.

C04 24/7 Snacks

cheese and quesadillas

A grilled cheese sandwich is pretty good, especially the one on page 58. I'm even down for a nice, hot pressed panino every now and then, especially from that place on Hudson and Grove. But my real go-to cheesy snack is, and always has been, a big gooey quesadilla. They're easy as hell to make, not to mention fast.

4   medium **flour tortillas**, soft taco size, about 8 inches in diameter

1½ cups shredded **Jack cheese**

2   small **chorizo sausages**, thinly sliced

chorizo

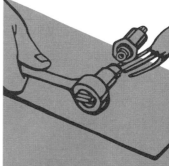

One at a time, place the tortillas directly on the stove burner over a gas flame or preheated electric element until lightly toasted on one side, about 30 seconds. Set aside.

Heat up a large sauté pan. Place a tortilla, toasted side up, into the sauté pan. Cook for 1 minute, then flip. Sprinkle one-fourth of the cheese over half of the tortilla. Add one-fourth of the chorizo. Fold the tortilla in half over the filling. Cook until the tortilla browns on the bottom, then flip, being careful not to lose your cheese. Brown the other side. The cheese should be melted by now. Repeat with the remaining tortillas. Eat while hot.

Doctor it up

What's your favorite kind of cheese? Cheddar? Muenster? Brie? Roquefort? And what, you like summer sausage better than chorizo? Change it up.

Serve this

When you're hungry *now*.

What to drink

If you're a Pepper, now's your big chance.

I like going to the movies. And I like popcorn. A lot. I really like Sour Patch Kids. And I love M&M's. But I don't like getting taken for an extra 10 bucks for concessions every time I go to the movies. So, putting cargo pockets to good use for a change, I now bring my own. Sweets in one pocket, savory in the other. Go ahead, call the cops on me.

FOR THE **SPICED NUTS**
AND **PRETZEL STICKS**

1   cup **unsalted peanuts, almonds,** and/or **pecans**

1   large handful of small **pretzel sticks** *(about ¾ cup)*

1   teaspoon **vegetable oil**

1   teaspoon **paprika**

1   teaspoon **garlic powder**

1   teaspoon **chile powder**

    Tabasco sauce to taste *(optional)*

FOR THE **COCOA KRISPIE POP-EMS**

3   tablespoons **unsalted butter**

1   bag *(about 10 ounces)* **marshmallows**

4   cups **Cocoa Krispies**

8   **peanut butter cups**, roughly chopped

movie

serves 2

make the spiced nuts and pretzel sticks

Preheat the oven to 375°F. Toss all the ingredients together in a medium bowl. Spread out on a baking sheet. Bake for 30 minutes. Let cool, then transfer to a paper bag.

make the Cocoa Krispie pop-ems

In the biggest microwave-safe bowl you have, zap the butter and marshmallows for 2 minutes. Stir and microwave for 30 more seconds. Stir in the Cocoa Krispies. Stir in peanut butter cups. Form into pop-em-size balls. Refrigerate on a baking sheet until firm, then transfer to a plastic bag.

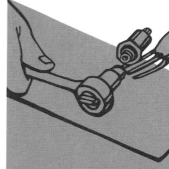

Doctor it up

Use plain Krispies and Whoppers in the pop-ems in place of Cocoa Krispies and peanut butter cups. Sweeten up the nuts with some sugar and lemon zest instead of paprika, garlic powder, and chile powder.

Serve this

After the previews end and the lights go down.

What to drink

A medium refillable Coke.

snacks

fancy snacks
for when you're
mixing martini

serves **6** to **8**

Let's face it. Not every night is a beer night. Some nights are martini nights. And those nights call for something a little higher-class than a bag of Fritos. The trick here is to buy tasty stuff, do very little to it, and make it look good on the plate. Puff pastry is in the freezer section of the supermarket. Don't be afraid. It's virtually un-fuck-up-able.

FOR THE **BAKED BRIE WITH QUINCE**

1 sheet slightly thawed **frozen puff pastry**

1 small round **Brie cheese**, about 7 to 10 ounces

¼ cup **quince preserves** (or apricot or orange or any flavor of preserves you want, but don't make it too sweet)

FOR THE **SPICED POTATO CHIPS**

1 bag (14 to 16 ounces) sturdy, high-end **potato chips** such as Cape Cod

1 tablespoon **smoked chile powder**

1 tablespoon **smoked paprika**

½ teaspoon **ground cumin**

FOR THE **ANTIPASTO PLATE**

½ pound **marinated black olives** (about 1 cup or so)

1½ pounds thinly sliced **cured meats** (such as prosciutto, speck, or soppressata) or **sausages**.

1 chunk (about 6 ounces) **Parmesan cheese**, broken up into bite-size bits

1 wedge (about 8 ounces) **soft cheese** (Find the best cheese store in your town, and ask the pro there for help. It's cool if it's the same Brie you're baking in the puff pastry.)

1 wedge (about 8 ounces) **aged sheep's milk cheese** (ditto as above, get the pro to help)

1 jar (about 10 ounces) **marinated roasted peppers, strained**

1 jar (about 10 ounces) **marinated artichoke hearts, strained**

1 box (about 1 pound) **imported breadsticks**

continued

make the baked brie

Preheat the oven to 350°F. Lay the puff pastry flat on a clean work surface. Center the cheese round on pastry and spread the preserves over the top. Fold the puff pastry up over the top of the Brie, trimming the excess and pressing together the seams. Bake for 25 minutes. Let cool slightly before serving.

make the spiced potato chips

Preheat the oven to 350°F. Open the bag of chips carefully along the top. Pour all the spices into the bag, then hold closed and shake. Pour the chips onto a baking sheet and bake for 10 minutes. *(This can be done during the last few minutes of your Brie-bake.)* Let cool.

make the antipasto plate

Assemble all the ingredients on a platter— and make it look nice.

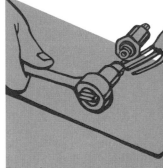

Doctor it up

Make a totally different antipasto plate. Hit the gourmet prepared-foods department at the grocery store—it's a gold mine for occasions like this. Take advantage: caponata, roasted vegetables, lamb chop lollipops, crudités, and plenty of cheese.

Serve this

To your best friends.

What to drink

Martinis. Not too dry, please *(vermouth is underrated)*, but plenty cold. Cocktail onion for garnish for me. Lemon twists or olives for others.

blender shake

Don't worry, you didn't lose consciousness and wake up reading some guide to Ripped Abs or Great Guns or anything. But sometimes, after a rough tennis match or long run, or, hell, even after the way you climbed the stairs today instead of taking the elevator all the way to 2, a restorative shake packed with vitamins is totally in order. This is a great snack, and a killer breakfast, too.

1   **banana**

1   tablespoon **honey**

1   tablespoon **smooth peanut butter**

½   cup **Cheerios** or other whole-grain cereal *(or oatmeal, but only use half as much or it'll go all gummy)*

1   small *(about 6 ounces)* **vanilla yogurt**

2   cups **low-fat milk**, soy milk, or water

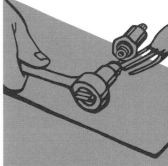

Put all the ingredients in a blender. Blend for 1 minute. Stop the blender, scrape down the sides with a rubber spatula, and blend for another 30 seconds, or until frothy.

Doctor it up

Add a package of protein-shake mix. Or some fruit. (Grapes. Pineapple. Raspberries. Mango. Papaya. Frozen peaches. Frozen blueberries. Dates. Melons. Whatever.)

Serve this

After your workout—not before.

What to drink

A glass of water and a multivitamin.

C04   24/7 Snacks

Some people like a really meaty nacho, one loaded up with beans and plenty of beef and chicken. I respect these people, but I don't concur with their nacho preferences. I like a lean, mean, cheesy, never soggy nacho with crunch, cheesiness, and heat, but no goop.

FOR THE SALSA FRESCA

3 **plum** *(Roma)* **tomatoes**, finely chopped

2 **green onions**, chopped

½ small **onion**, chopped

2 **garlic cloves**, smashed and minced

Leaves of ½ bunch **fresh cilantro**, chopped

½ cup **corn kernels**, thawed frozen or shaved from 1 ear *(cooked or raw)*

2 small **jalapeño chiles**, finely chopped *(seeds and pith removed for less heat)*

Juice of 1 **lime**

Pinch of **salt**

FOR THE GUACAMOLE

2 large, ripe **avocados** *(you can tell if an avocado's ready if pressing on it leaves a faint imprint of your grubby thumb)*

½ small **onion**, diced

1 small **jalapeño chile**, chopped

1 small **tomato**, chopped

Juice of 1 **lime**, 1 teaspoon reserved for garnish

Leaves of ½ bunch **fresh cilantro**, chopped

FOR THE NACHOS

1 large bag *(about 10 ounces)* **tortilla chips**

1 cup shredded **Cheddar cheese**

1 cup shredded **Monterey Jack cheese**

1 small can *(about 5 ounces)* **jalapeño peppers**, drained and finely chopped

1 tablespoon **dried minced onions**

nachos

make the salsa fresca

Mix together all the ingredients in a bowl.
Taste and adjust the ingredients to your taste.
Transfer to a serving bowl.

make the guacamole

Peel and pit the avocados by slicing in half
around the pit, then pulling the halves apart.
Scoop out the flesh and place in a large bowl.
Using a couple of knives, mash together
the avocado, onion, jalapeño, tomato, lime
juice, and cilantro until roughly combined.
Transfer to a large serving bowl, then sprinkle
the 1 teaspoon reserved lime juice over the top.
*(This will keep your guac from turning brown
before you finish with your nachos.)*

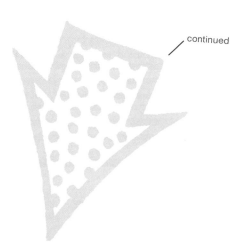

continued

make the nachos

Preheat the oven to 500°F. Spread the tortilla chips out on a baking sheet. Sprinkle the cheeses evenly over the top. Sprinkle the jalapeños and minced onions evenly on top of the cheese. Bake for 5 minutes, then turn on the broiler and slide the nachos under it. Broil for 2 minutes. Serve hot, straight from the baking sheet, spooning salsa fresca and guacamole onto the chips as you eat.

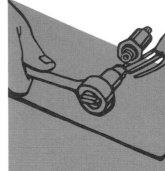

Doctor it up

Hey, if you wanna add a premium tequila floater to your salsa, who am I to say *"¡Ay, pero no!"*

Serve this

I find this to be a good-luck dish when I'm watching the U.S. Open. Go Roddick.

What to drink

A shot of mezcal, followed by your favorite Mexican beer.

chile powder popcorn

Somewhere in this great land of ours, I'm sure there's someone who's marketing BBQ popcorn. It's too good an idea not to make money off of. But whoever that is, I bet mine is better.

½ cup **unpopped yellow popcorn**

1 to 2 teaspoons **chile powder**
(Use a single standard powder, or make your own mix, to your taste. Many Mexican specialty stores will have several to choose from.)

½ teaspoon **table salt** *(sea salt or kosher salt will be too coarse)*

1½ teaspoons **vegetable oil**

continued

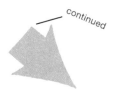

In a small bowl, stir together the popcorn, chile powder, and salt. In a large covered saucepan, soup pot, or enameled Dutch oven with a tight-fitting lid, heat the oil over high heat. Drop in one popcorn kernel. When it pops, the oil is ready. Pour the popcorn into the pot. Cover and shake the pot back and forth to make sure popcorn is coated with oil and chile powder. Allow the popcorn to pop until the popping slows dramatically to about one pop every 3 seconds. Remove from the heat immediately. When popping stops, remove the lid. Give the popcorn a quick stir. Taste it, and add more chile powder or salt if you want.

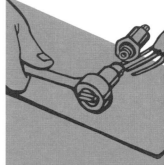

Doctor it up

Try cumin. Try garlic powder. Try paprika. Try cinnamon. Try black pepper. They'll all work.

Serve this

When your TiVo is full and you need to clear out some space.

What to drink

Call me crazy, but I like a martini with my popcorn. To be fair, I like a martini with anything.

05

salads a

salad? uh, can i have fries instead?

Let me start this chapter by coming clean: Salad annoys me. Nothing depresses me more than reading a menu and seeing "comes with a complimentary small garden salad"—except maybe an All-You-Can-Eat salad bar. I mean, can we all be honest? Who wants to stuff themselves cross-eyed on a bunch of iceberg lettuce, limp red radishes, and cucumber slices? And don't get me started on fake bacon bits. Guaranteed, no one goes home happy from one of those.

Luckily, there's more to salad. I'm talking about cheese *(real cheese)*, bacon *(real bacon)*, and killer dressings. And sometimes, even greens. And believe it or not, or care or not: Greens are good for you.

As for soup, I love soup. Everyone loves soup. Especially homemade soup. If you don't love homemade soup, you need your head checked.

Now, you can make your own. And trust me, it's worth it. Make it for yourself, and you'll be happy. Make it for someone else, and they'll always come back for more.

nd soups

hot

Double this recipe if you've got more than four people to feed, or if you want leftovers—which you do, because this salad tastes even better the next day, and even better the day after that. Eat it cold straight out of the fridge, or warm it up again and serve it with ketchup. This salad is easy, but it's got a lot of moving parts. Get the potatoes going first, but stay on top of them, or they'll overcook and turn to mush.

3 pounds small **red potatoes,** scrubbed but not peeled, halved

2 tablespoons **salt**

4 **eggs**

1 pound **bacon strips**

1 small **red onion,** finely chopped

1 bunch **green onions,** white parts and about half of the green parts, chopped

1 small **green** or **red** or **yellow bell pepper,** seeded and finely chopped

   Capers to taste (if you like them)

¼ cup **red wine vinegar**

   Juice of 1 **lemon**

2 tablespoons **country-style** (whole-grain) **mustard**

2 tablespoons **mayonnaise**

In a large pot, cover the potatoes with cold water, allowing about 1 inch of water above the potatoes. Add the salt. Bring to a boil over high heat. Boil for 20 minutes, or until just tender when you pierce one with a fork. Do not overcook. Drain into a colander, but do not rinse.

Place the eggs in a small saucepan under just enough cold water to cover. Bring to a boil, then cover tightly and remove from the heat. Let stand in the hot water for 10 minutes, then peel under cold running water. Place in a bowl of cold water until ready to use.

potato salad

Meanwhile, in a large sauté pan, cook the bacon in batches over medium heat, transferring each batch when finished to a stack of paper towels to crisp. Reserve the bacon drippings from each batch in a heatproof bowl or dish. Once crispy, break the bacon up into 1-inch pieces.

Return about ¼ cup of the bacon drippings to the pan along with the red onion, green onions, bell pepper, and capers, if using. Cook for 2 minutes, the lower heat to medium. Add the red wine vinegar and lemon juice, being careful not to splatter. Scrape up the brown bits from the bottom of the pan and stir to incorporate them into the liquid. Bring to a boil and let bubble for 1 minute.

Remove from the heat. Whisk in the mustard and mayonnaise. Shake away any excess water from the potatoes and add to the sauté pan. Toss to coat. Spoon the potatoes into a serving bowl, pouring the dressing left in the pan over all, if you want to. Drain and pat dry the eggs, quarter them, and add them to the bowl, tossing lightly to coat. Serve warm.

Doctor it up

Add ¼ cup of paprika to turn it red, and hot.

Serve this

Next to a grilled cheeseburger.

What to drink

A cold Czech pilsner.

salad of cheese and bacon (chopped cobb)

serves **1** to **2**

Sure, everyone knows the story of the Caesar salad and how it was invented by some guy in Tijuana named Caesar. But let's raise our iced teas in a toast to Robert Cobb, a ridiculously intelligent man from Los Angeles who, back in the 1930s, ran the Brown Derby restaurant, where he changed everything we thought we knew about salads. By installing bacon and cheese and eggs next to all that lettuce, he succeeded in creating what is, for many, the Holy Grail of salads–one that tastes nothing like salad and everything like a BLT with Roquefort. When you're assembling this salad, taste each ingredient individually, and decide how much to add based on what tastes good. As with all salads, if you don't like one of the ingredients I've listed, go to Hell. Just kidding.

½ pound **bacon strips**

FOR THE **DRESSING**

¼ cup **red wine vinegar**

2 teaspoons **Dijon mustard** *(country-style is cool, but classic is better)*

2 tablespoons **rendered bacon fat** *(from the bacon you'll cook first)*

½ cup **olive oil**

Juice of ½ **lemon**

Freshly ground **black pepper**

FOR THE **SALAD**

2 large **eggs**

1 small head **Romaine lettuce**, cored and chopped

½ head **iceberg lettuce**, cored and chopped

½ bunch **watercress**, tough stems removed, chopped

8 to 10 leaves **red leaf lettuce**, chopped

1 large, ripe **tomato** *(If it's mid-winter and the tomatoes in your supermarket suck, blow it off. Bad tomatoes are definitely not worth it.)*

3 **green onions**, chopped

1 large, ripe **avocado**, pitted, peeled, and cubed

A few crumbles of **blue cheese**

continued

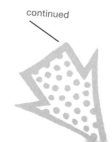

Snip the bacon into bite-size pieces. Sauté in a frying pan over medium-high heat until crispy. Remove to paper towels to drain. Save 2 tablespoons of the bacon fat for the dressing and discard the rest.

make the dressing

Put all the ingredients in a jar with a tight-fitting lid, screw on the lid tightly, and shake until emulsified. Taste and adjust the seasoning if you want. Shake again.

make the salad

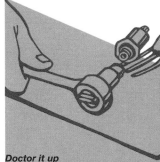

Place the eggs in a small saucepan under just enough cold water to cover. Bring to a boil, then cover tightly and remove from the heat. Let stand in the hot water for 10 minutes, then peel under cold running water. Place in a bowl of cold water until ready to use.

Put the chopped greens, tomato, and green onions in a large bowl. Add the bacon pieces. Toss them around with a pair of tongs, then add about half of the dressing. Toss again to coat everything. Continue adding more drizzles of dressing until everything's just coated. *(Too much dressing ruins a salad. I know this sounds like blasphemy, but it's true. Add more dressing later if you must, but don't drown it now.)*

Drain and dry the eggs, then chop coarsely. Throw the avocado, eggs, and cheese over the top of the salad and eat. *(I usually chow it straight from the bowl I made it in.)*

Doctor it up

Next time, for a smoky flavor, before you chop up the romaine, slice the heart down the middle lengthwise and grill it in a stovetop grill pan *(or out on the grill if you have one, you lucky bastard)* for 3 minutes per side. Yum.

Serve this

When you're feeling virtuous but also hungry. And believe it or not, this is one of the few salads that makes OK leftovers, for about one day.

What to drink

A cold glass of Sauvignon Blanc or a glass of cold iced tea.

spanish fly salad
(hold the fly)

I wish I could tell you that this salad will, without question, improve your sex life. But I can't. Nothing that you eat is *guaranteed* to keep you at attention next time you're, uh, on the spot unless it's blue and diamond-shaped and taken with water. But this salad is packed full of vitamins that count, and that can't hurt.

FOR THE **DRESSING**

2 tablespoons **red wine vinegar**

½ teaspoon **dry mustard**

1 tablespoon **mayonnaise**

½ teaspoon **paprika**

Juice of ½ **lemon**

¾ cup **olive oil**

Salt and **pepper**

FOR THE **SALAD**

6 to 8 small **red potatoes** *(each bigger than a golf ball, but smaller than your fist)*, scrubbed but not peeled

2 tablespoons **salt**

2 **eggs**

1 bag *(about 5 ounces)* **baby spinach leaves**, unopened

½ cup **red beans**, drained, or more if you like them

1 large or 2 small **sweet green Italian frying peppers**, such as cubanelles

4 **anchovy fillets** *(optional if you suck)*

2 small **plum** *(Roma)* **tomatoes**, chopped *(if the tomatoes look bad in the store, skip it)*

continued

make the dressing

Put all the ingredients in a jar with a tight-fitting lid. Screw on the lid tightly and shake until emulsified. Taste and adjust the seasoning. Shake again.

make the salad

In a large pot, cover the potatoes with cold water, allowing about 1 inch of water above the potatoes. Add the salt. Bring to a boil over high heat. Boil for 20 minutes, or until just tender when you pierce one with a fork. Do not overcook. Drain into a colander, but do not rinse.

Place the eggs in a small saucepan under just enough cold water to cover. Bring to a boil, then cover tightly and remove from the heat. Let stand in the hot water for 10 minutes, then peel under cold running water. Place in a bowl of cold water until ready to use.

Pierce the plastic bag of spinach with a knife in 3 or 4 places. Microwave on high for 30 seconds. The leaves should be warm and beginning to wilt. Shake the bag and microwave for 5 seconds more. The leaves should be just wilted but not cooked through.

Arrange the salads on 2 plates in 4 quadrants: Northwest quadrant gets the spinach. Northeast takes beans and peppers. Southwest, potatoes and anchovies. Southeast, 1 hard-boiled egg, quartered. Tomatoes and olives sit in the middle. Shake the dressing again, then drizzle over the top.

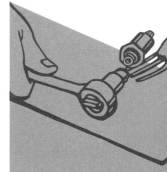

Doctor it up

Call me unoriginal and throw on some bacon. You know you want it.

Serve this

Before, or after, a weekend afternoon session. Or on a picnic: Prepare all the parts and transport them separately, then assemble the salads on the spot.

What to drink

The best cheap Spanish Rioja that your local vintner stocks.

wedgie with croutons

In terms of flavor, iceberg lettuce pretty much sucks. But its crunch pretty much rules. So, based on the idea that it's easier to improve the flavor of a crisp head of lettuce than it is to make a tastier bunch of greens crisp, someone invented the iceberg-wedge-with-blue-cheese salad. My take on it is only a semi-ripoff, with no blue cheese in sight.

FOR THE **CROUTONS**

1 teaspoon **garlic powder**

3 tablespoons **olive oil**

2 tablespoons **unsalted butter**

1 tablespoon **paprika**

½ loaf **rustic bread** *(sourdough or country white)*, at least a day old, crusts removed and cut into 1-inch cubes

¼ cup grated **Parmesan cheese**

FOR THE **DRESSING**

¼ cup **sour cream**

¼ cup **mayonnaise**

2 tablespoons **ketchup**

Juice of ½ **lemon**

1 to 2 tablespoons **chile powder** *(start with 1, then add more if you want)*

Salt

Olive oil, if needed

1 head fresh, crisp **iceberg lettuce**

8 stalks **green onions**, trimmed and halved lengthwise

continued

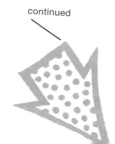

make the croutons

Preheat the oven to 350°F. Combine the garlic powder, olive oil, butter, and paprika in a large ovenproof sauté pan and warm over low heat for 10 minutes. Remove pan from the heat, add the bread cubes and cheese, and stir to coat. Throw the sauté pan in the oven for about 15 minutes; don't leave it in there too long. Golden and crispy, maybe a little bit brown, is what you're looking for. Burnt bread is no good, so toss it and start over if you need to.

make the dressing

Whisk together all the ingredients. If the dressing is too thick, add a drop or two of olive oil. Remember to taste and adjust the seasonings.

Slice the lettuce into 4 wedges, leaving the stem end intact. Put 2 wedges on each of 2 plates and top each with half of the green onions. Garnish with the croutons and drizzle plenty of the dressing over the top.

Doctor it up

Get rid of the chile powder in the dressing and use dry mustard and minced dried onion instead. Or whatever the hell else blows your skirt up.

Serve this

Alongside a plate of buffalo wings.

What to drink

Take your pick: a sharp Italian Pinot Grigio or an icy beer.

bloody mary tomato soup

Two of the greatest inventions in human history: tomato soup and the Bloody Mary. Like Reese's peanut butter cups, two great tastes that taste great together. Believe it or not, it's all about the clam juice in this recipe. Even though you can't really taste the clam, it really makes the cocktailness of it all.

8   **plum** *(Roma)* **tomatoes**

1   medium **onion**

    Salt and **pepper**

2   teaspoons **olive oil**, plus more for drizzling

2   stalks **celery**, chopped

2   **garlic cloves**, chopped

1   teaspoon **red pepper flakes**

1   **bay leaf**

2   cups **chicken stock** *(page 108)*, or canned chicken or vegetable broth, or water

1   cup **bottled clam juice**

    A couple pinches of **celery seed**

¼   teaspoon **prepared horseradish** *(you'll know it's prepared because it's in a jar)*

    Tabasco sauce to taste

    Lemon zest to taste

4   shots of **vodka**

continued

Preheat the oven to 350°F. Cut the tomatoes into quarters and toss into a roasting pan. Spread them out so there's only one layer. Quarter the onion and throw it in, too. Add a pinch of salt and a few grindings of pepper, then drizzle olive oil over all. Roast for about 40 to 45 minutes, stirring once or twice. Remove from the oven and pick the tomato skins out with tongs *(they should slide off easily)*.

In a large saucepan over medium-high heat, heat the olive oil and sauté the celery, garlic, and red pepper flakes until fragrant. Don't burn the garlic. Add the bay leaf and sauté for 1 minute. Add the roasted tomatoes and onions to the pot, then the chicken stock and clam juice. Bring to a boil, then drop the heat and simmer the soup for 30 minutes. *(If you're smart, you'll get out the fixin's for some grilled cheese sandwiches, page 58, in the meantime.)* Remove soup from the heat and let cool down a little. Taste the soup and adjust the seasonings if you need to. Fish out the bay leaf.

Using a handheld blender *(a.k.a. immersion blender)*, purée the soup thoroughly. Or, transfer the soup to a standing blender and purée. *(Work in batches. Overfill that blender with hot soup and you'll be wearing it.)*

Return the soup to the saucepan and reheat if necessary. Pour into soup bowls and sprinkle with the celery seed, horseradish, Tabasco, and lemon zest. Float a vodka shot on top of each.

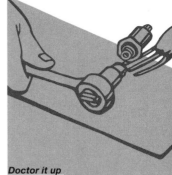

Doctor it up

Toss in some fresh lump crabmeat. Yum. Or, corn kernels. Or peas. Yum.

Serve this

For dinner The Day After. This soup banishes all traces of a hangover.

What to drink

Redundant.

joe mama's

Believe this, if you believe nothing else I say: It is easy to make chicken soup. In fact, it's easy to make really *good* chicken soup—even if you have a raging cold. And homemade soup is about a thousand times better than anything you'll find in a can. And take this tip: make extra stock to have on hand. Just double or triple the stock part of this recipe and freeze it in airtight containers *(hello, Tupperware)* for up to 3 months. Almost all soups and sauces are better when you use homemade chicken stock in the base. Pasta boiled in chicken stock tastes way better than regular pasta. Vegetables steamed in just a couple tablespoons of stock taste way better. *(Freeze the stock in ice cube trays for this so it's premeasured.)*

FOR THE STOCK

1 **chicken**, cut into 8 parts *(Buy it already cut up, or hack away at it yourself: 2 wings, 2 legs, 2 thighs, 2 breasts. To lighten your grocery bill and just make the stock and not soup, skip the whole chicken and use chicken parts like wings and backs and necks instead.)*

1 large **onion**, quartered

1 large **carrot**, peeled and coarsely chopped

2 stalks **celery**, coarsely chopped

1 **bay leaf**

1 teaspoon **whole peppercorns**

Pinch of **salt** *(don't use any more than this)*

FOR THE SOUP

2 teaspoons **olive oil**

1 medium **onion**, sliced

1 large **carrot**, peeled and chopped

1 stalk **celery**, chopped

2 **garlic cloves**, chopped

1 pound **russet potatoes**, scrubbed and cubed *(peeling optional)*

Pinch of **red pepper flakes**

1 bag *(about 5 ounces)* **baby spinach**

108

chicken soup

make the stock

Put all the stock ingredients in a soup pot. Add cold water to cover. Bring to a boil, then lower the heat to simmer for 2 hours. *(Don't bother skimming the foam from your soup while it's simmering, unless you're being tested on it later. It's no big deal.)* Using a slotted spoon, transfer the chicken pieces to a plate. Remove the vegetables and bay leaf and throw them out. Strain stock through a fine-mesh sieve, discarding the peppercorns and other solids. *(If you're making chicken stock for another recipe, or to freeze, stop here. If you're doing the full-on chicken soup, keep going.)*

make the soup

Tear the chicken meat from the bones. In a medium saucepan over high heat, warm the olive oil. Add the onion, carrot, celery, garlic, and potatoes and sauté for 3 minutes. Add the red pepper flakes and stir. Add 6 cups chicken stock *(if you're short on stock, top it off with water)* and bring to a low boil. Add the chicken meat and simmer for 15 min-utes, or until the potatoes are tender. Add the spinach and stir it into the soup. It'll wilt quickly, in just a minute or two, and when it does, serve the soup immediately.

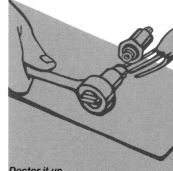

Doctor it up

Ditch the red pepper flakes and use a couple tablespoons of chile powder for a smokier soup. Or ditch the flakes and spinach and use freshly grated ginger and a few sprigs of watercress for a more Asian soup.

Serve this

When you feel like shit.

What to drink

Ginger ale.

Baked French onion soup with a bread-and-Gruyère topping is one of my favorite things in the world to eat, but it's usually best left to restaurants that also serve 740 types of imported beer. When I'm at home, I dig this version. It's really easy, and the egg really makes it happen.

2	tablespoons **unsalted butter**
2	tablespoons **olive oil**
4	**yellow onions**, sliced into rings
	Salt and **pepper**
3	**garlic cloves**, minced
1	**bay leaf**
2	teaspoons **dried tarragon**
2	tablespoons **Dijon mustard**

3½ to 4 cups **prepared beef broth** *(or vegetable broth, but it will taste much, much different)*

3 cups fresh **cold water**, or more if needed

4 **eggs**

1 can *(about 3 ounces)* **crispy fried onions** *(the kind people put on green bean casserole)*

serves 4

fried onion
with poach

Melt the butter with the olive oil in a large soup pot over medium heat, then add the onions and a pinch each of salt and pepper. Sauté until the onions are soft, brown, and caramelized, about 30 minutes. Don't rush this step. Add the garlic, bay leaf, and tarragon, raise the heat to high, and sauté for 2 minutes. Whisk in the mustard, then add the broth and water. Bring the soup up to a boil, reduce the heat to medium again, and simmer for 30 minutes.

A few minutes before you're ready to serve, fish out the bay leaf. Taste the soup and adjust the seasonings if you need to. Crack the eggs, one at a time, into the gently simmering soup to poach. *(Tip: Break them one by one into a small bowl first, then slide them carefully into the soup to avoid getting shells in your soup.)* Poach for about 4 to 5 minutes, until the eggs are set but the yolks are still runny.

Ladle the soup into bowls, making sure each bowl gets an egg. Sprinkle the crispy onions over the top. Eat immediately; your egg yolk should run all through the soup.

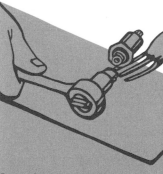

Doctor it up

Crumbled bacon, a few croutons, a few stalks of sautéed broccoli raab. Live it up.

Serve this

On rainy nights.

What to drink

A thick French Bordeaux.

soup
ed egg

the ramen that a meal

eats like

You always knew, somewhere in the back of your mind, that even though ramen noodles are the cheapest thing at the grocery store *(at 3 to 5 packages for a dollar in most towns, they leave mac-n-cheese in the dust)*, they're also actually really good. Follow this recipe exactly if you must, or better yet, jack it up any old way you feel like—mushrooms, parsley, bok choy, ginger, sausages, shrimp, Cajun spices, even a splash of sherry.

1   **pre-cooked boneless chicken breast** from the deli counter

1   teaspoon **olive oil**

1   stalk **celery**, finely chopped

1   **carrot**, peeled and shredded

1   tablespoon **Dijon mustard**

   Pinch of **salt**

2   cups **chicken stock** *(page 108)* or canned broth

2½ cups **water**

   Pinch of **red pepper flakes**

2   packages *(about 3 ounces each)* **ramen noodles** *(Choose any flavor. It doesn't matter 'cause you're not going to use that crappy little seasoning packet anyway.)*

2   large **eggs**, lightly beaten

1   bag *(about 5 ounces)* **baby spinach**

1   teaspoon peeled and grated **fresh ginger**

1   **green onion**, chopped

continued

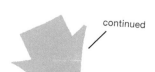

Chop up the chicken into small cubes. In a medium saucepan over medium-high heat, warm the olive oil. Add the chicken, celery, carrot, mustard, and salt and sauté until the celery and carrot are soft, about 3 minutes. Add the chicken stock and water, turn up the heat to high, and bring to a boil. As soon as it boils, turn down the heat to medium-low, cover, and simmer for 5 more minutes. Add the red pepper flakes.

Crank the heat back up to high, drop in the ramen blocks, and cover the pan. Lower the heat to medium-low and let simmer for 2 minutes.

Uncover and stir. Your noodles should be pretty much cooked. While you're stirring, pour in your beaten eggs in a slow stream, stirring while you pour. You want the egg to get distributed throughout the soup. If you do it right, it should create strings of egg in the soup. If you don't do it right, it will still taste delicious.

Add the spinach, pushing the leaves down into the soup. It'll seem like you have way too much spinach, but trust me, it'll practically disappear. Cover and simmer until the leaves are wilted, about 1 to 2 minutes. Stir in the ginger.

Remove from the heat. Serve hot, garnished with chopped green onion.

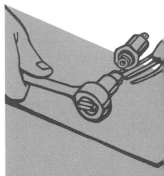

Doctor it up

Add some chopped bacon, half a box of frozen corn niblets or frozen peas, some chopped broccoli or eggplant. Try coconut milk, a little curry powder, some cumin, chile sauce. Or drop a cracked egg into the broth while it's still simmering, poaching it right in the soup: Cook for 2½ minutes, then remove from the heat and serve immediately. The yolk, when you pierce it, should be runny so it melts into the soup.

Serve this

The last Thursday before payday.

What to drink

Your favorite Asian beer. Sapporo, Tsingtao, Tiger, your call.

pasta e fagiole

Some soups, like this one, taste way better when you start with both butter and olive oil. The butter adds a little nuttiness to the mix, which makes those beans all that much more satisfying. This is the perfect soup for re-viewing your *Sopranos* DVDs. Have your first bowl of this right after you make it, when the vegetables are still crisp. Then have a bowl tomorrow, after they've softened up.

2   tablespoons **unsalted butter**

2   tablespoons **olive oil**

1   **onion**, chopped

1   **carrot**, peeled and chopped

1   stalk **celery**, chopped

2   **garlic cloves**, smashed and
     finely chopped

     Pinch of **salt**

     freshly ground **black pepper**

1   bay leaf

continued

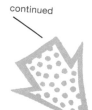

4 cups **chicken stock** *(page 108)* or canned broth

1 can *(about 14.5 ounces)* **diced tomatoes**, with their juice

1 tablespoon **ketchup**

1 can *(about 15½ ounces)* **white beans** such as cannellini or Great Northern

½ pound **spaghetti**, broken into pieces 3 to 4 inches long

1 bag *(about 5 ounces)* **baby spinach leaves**

In a soup pot over high heat, melt the butter with the olive oil. Add the onion, carrot, celery, garlic, salt, and pepper to taste and sauté until the vegetables are soft.

Add the bay leaf, chicken stock, tomatoes and juice, ketchup, and white beans. Bring to a boil, then reduce the heat to medium-low and simmer for 15 minutes. Add the pasta and simmer for 10 minutes more. Fish out the bay leaf. Taste and adjust the seasoning. Add the spinach. As soon as it wilts, your soup is ready.

Doctor it up

Hey, it's soup. Throw whatever the hell you want in there, I don't care.

Serve this

When it's too late to order in.

What to drink

An Italian red table wine.

Gentlemen, Start Your Ovens

06

supp

supper is the king of meals.

I've made it clear just how deeply I love breakfast, one of my most favorite meals. *(Just see Chapter 2.)* And lunch, well, lunch is irreplaceable, a true giant in the pantheon of daily repasts. But in my book *(which this is)*, let there be no question: Supper is king.

It has the distinct advantage, the insurmountable advantage, of coming at the end of the day. When you sit down to supper, the workday is over, you're not on the clock, and you're not likely anxious to do much of anything strenuous afterwards. With supper, you can relax, which means that you can really taste and enjoy it.

Take your time making supper if you can, even if it's a simple recipe. Crack a beer or pour a glass of wine *(or, hell, Jack on the rocks)*, find some good tunes, and fire up your oven. A few swipes of the knife and swirls of the whisk later, and you'll be sitting pretty, a fat plate of goodness in front of you. And that's a happy seat to sit in.

I am all about leftovers, so most of these recipes make enough for a couple midnight forkfuls, maybe even a nice lunch tomorrow.

steak, champ
serves 1

Why complicate things, when a steak fried in butter is one of the greatest meals there is? The keys here are a good steak and a hot pan. *(Always make sure you're getting the best available at the butcher. 'Cause if you don't, someone else will.)* And for chrissakes, please don't overcook it. Medium-rare *(pink in the middle, charred on the outside)* is perfect. And to go with it? It's hard to beat a package of frozen shoestring potatoes. But if you've got a couple extra minutes, whip up this combo of mashed potatoes with green onions, a.k.a. champ.

FOR THE **CHAMP**

2   medium to large **russet potatoes**, peeled

4   **green onions**, chopped

½   cup **milk**

4   tablespoons *(½ stick)* **unsalted butter**

Salt and **pepper**

2   tablespoons **unsalted butter**, plus extra for garnish

Scant teaspoon of **olive oil**

1   **rib-eye steak**, about 8 to 10 ounces and about ½ inch thick

½   glass **red wine**, or ⅓ cup chicken stock *(page 108)* or canned broth or water

continued

make the champ

Chop the potatoes into ½-inch cubes, about the size of playing dice. Toss into a medium saucepan and cover with cold water. Bring to a boil. Boil for 15 minutes, or until potatoes are soft but not yet gummy. While the potatoes are cooking, mix the green onions, milk, and butter in a microwave-safe bowl. Zap for 1 minute, stir, and zap for 30 seconds more. Drain the potatoes and place in a large bowl. Stir in the green-onion mixture slowly. You may not need it all. Mash everything together. The champ should definitely be mushier and runnier than mashed potatoes, but not soupy. Season well with salt and pepper.

C06 Supper

121

Open the windows and turn on the fan. In a medium sauté pan over high heat, heat the 2 tablespoons butter with the olive oil just until it smokes. Lay the steak carefully into the pan, making sure the entire bottom surface is in contact with the metal. Do not touch it for 3 minutes. Using tongs, flip the steak to brown the other side. Again, lay off it and let it cook for 3 more minutes without touching it. Flip it back, cook for 1 more minute, then transfer to a cutting board and let rest for 5 minutes. Meanwhile, still over high heat, add the wine and scrape up the browned bits from the bottom of the pan into the liquid. Boil hard for 3 to 4 minutes, until the liquid is reduced by half. Remove from the heat.

Spoon the champ onto a plate, covering the bottom of the plate. Drop your steak on top. Place a large pat of butter, like a tablespoon, on top of your steak, then pour the pan sauce over the butter.

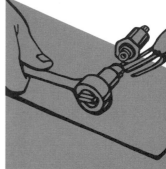

Doctor it up

After you remove the steak, add a shot of bourbon to the pan. Cook the bourbon until it evaporates, then add the liquid and reduce as above. Or, whisk a teaspoon or two of Dijon mustard into the pan sauce just before pouring it over the steak. Doctor up the champ with a clove of garlic, smashed and chopped, or by sautéing the green onions in the butter instead of the microwave step.

Serve this

When it's Boy's Night In *(solo)*.

What to drink

A solid New Zealand Pinot Noir.

meat loaf

Meat loaf is a staple at my place. It's almost impossible to fuck it up, and it makes the best sandwiches known to man. Some people make meat loaf with just beef, or just beef and pork, or just turkey *(which can be surprisingly good)*, but the Holy Trifecta of beef, pork, and veal is impossible to beat.

3   slices day-old or stale **bread** or ⅓ French baguette, torn into small pieces

1   cup **milk**

½   pound **bacon slices**

1   teaspoon **olive oil**

1   medium **onion**, diced

1   medium **carrot**, peeled and diced

2   stalks **celery**, diced

2   **garlic cloves**, smashed and minced

½   pound **ground beef**, about 80 percent lean

½   pound **ground pork**

½   pound **ground veal**

2   teaspoons **salt**

2   teaspoons **pepper**

2   **eggs**, lightly beaten

⅓   cup **ketchup**, plus extra for serving

¼   cup **Dijon mustard**

¼   cup grated **Parmesan cheese** *(preferably Parmigiano-Reggiano)*

continued

Preheat the oven to 350°F. In a small bowl, soak the torn bread in the milk for a few minutes.

While the bread is soaking, cut 1 bacon slice into small pieces. Sauté with the olive oil in a medium saucepan over medium-high heat until the fat has rendered. Add the onion, carrot, and celery and sauté for 5 minutes, or until the vegetables are soft. Add the garlic and sauté for 2 minutes more, then remove from the heat. Transfer the vegetables to a bowl to cool.

In a large mixing bowl, use your hands to combine the beef, pork, and veal with the salt and pepper. Add the eggs, ketchup, mustard, and cheese. Pick the bread out of the milk and squeeze out the excess milk into a small bowl. Squish the bread into the meat mixture. Add the cooled vegetables and combine. The meat mixture should be pretty gooey. Add some of the squeezed bread-milk if you need more moisture.

Form the mixture into a loaf on a baking sheet lined with aluminum foil. Drape the remaining bacon slices over the top of the loaf. Bake for 40 minutes, or until an instant-read thermometer registers 150°F. Let your meat loaf loaf for 10 minutes or so before slicing into it. Serve with lots of ketchup.

Doctor it up

Add some sausage meat to the mix. Just slice open the casings and remove the filling. Or, ditch the Parmesan and add dried herbs like tarragon or thyme.

Serve this

Meat loaf is always on time. Serve it any season, any night.

What to drink

Give this loaf some love and pick yourself up a fine Australian Shiraz.

meatball three-way (or moreway)

Bite-sized kissing cousins of the meat loaf on page 123, meatballs are, quite simply, a perfect food. You can use them on sandwiches *(see page 62)*, in pasta *(see page 144)*, in soup, or all by their tasty little selves. Here I'm giving up one base recipe with three different flavor directions to try. It's a good idea to make a bunch of meatballs, then freeze them. They'll keep, uncooked and bagged in bunches of six, for a couple of months in a deep-freeze. When you're ready to use them, let them thaw for a half-hour or so while you have a beer, then proceed according to the cooking directions below.

BASE MEATBALL

3 slices day-old or stale **bread** or ⅓ French baguette, torn into small pieces

1 cup **milk**

1 **bacon slice**

1 teaspoon **olive oil**

1 medium **onion**, diced

1 medium **carrot**, peeled and diced

2 stalks **celery**, diced

½ pound **ground beef**, about 80 percent lean

½ pound **ground pork**

½ pound **ground veal**

2 teaspoons **salt**

2 teaspoons **pepper**

2 **eggs**, lightly beaten

continued

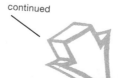

FOR **ITALIAN MEATBALLS**

⅓ cup **ketchup**

1 small can *(about 6 ounces)* **tomato paste**

2 **garlic cloves**, smashed and minced

1 tablespoon **dried oregano**

About 2 cups of your favorite **tomato sauce**, or make the one on page 144

FOR **GERMAN MEATBALLS**

2 tablespoons **paprika**

A few gratings of **nutmeg**

2 teaspoons **Worcestershire sauce**

1 cup **chicken stock** *(page 108)* or canned unsalted broth, or as needed

Leftover **milk** from when you soaked the bread

FOR **ASIAN MEATBALLS**

1 tablespoon **ground ginger**

3 tablespoons **low-sodium soy sauce** *(Trust me. If you use regular, you'll be hating it.)*

2 **garlic cloves**, smashed and minced

2 tablespoons **sesame oil**

2 tablespoons **Dijon mustard**

3 **green onions**, sliced

4 cups **chicken stock** *(page 108)* or canned broth, plus extra *(or added water)* if needed

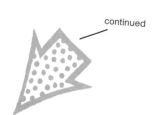

continued

make the base

In a small bowl, soak the torn bread in the milk for a few minutes.

While the bread is soaking, cut the bacon into small pieces. Sauté with the olive oil in a medium saucepan over medium-high heat until the fat has rendered. Add the onion, carrot, and celery and sauté for 5 minutes, or until the vegetables are soft. Transfer the vegetables to a bowl to cool.

In a large mixing bowl, use your hands to combine the beef, pork, and veal with the salt and pepper. Add the eggs. Pick the bread out of the milk and squeeze out the excess milk, reserving the milk. Squish the bread into the meat mixture. Add the cooled vegetables and combine. The meat mixture should be pretty gooey. Add some of the squeezed bread-milk if you need more moisture.

To make plain old meatballs, preheat the oven to 450°F. Form the mixture into balls 1 to 1½ inches in diameter. Arrange on a baking sheet with at least two inches between each ball. Slide in oven, immediately reduce heat to 350°F, and bake for 20 minutes.

For any of the variations below, don't add any of the excess milk squeezed from the bread until everything's in the mix; it'll probably be moist enough without it. But if you need more moisture, use the milk.

for italian meatballs

Add all the Italian-meatball ingredients except the tomato sauce to the meatball base and combine. Form the mixture into balls about 1 to 1½ inches in diameter. In a sauté pan, warm up the tomato sauce to a low simmer, add the meatballs, and cook for 20 minutes. Serve over spaghetti, or over a plate of arugula if your khakis are feeling snug this week.

for german meatballs

Preheat the oven to 350°F. Add the paprika, nutmeg, and Worcestershire sauce to the meatball base and combine. Form the mixture into balls about 1 to 1½ inches in diameter. Sauté the meatballs in a large, ovenproof sauté pan until browned. Pour in the chicken stock, enough to cover the meatballs halfway. Top off with the reserved bread-milk. Working around the meatballs, scrape the bottom of the pan to release brown bits. Slide the sauté pan into oven and bake for 20 minutes, checking liquid level halfway through cooking. Add a little more chicken stock if necessary to keep the meatballs half submerged. Serve over wide noodles, or cabbage *(see khaki suggestion above)*.

for asian meatballs

Add all the Asian-meatball ingredients except the chicken stock to the meatball base and combine. Form the mixture into balls about 1 to 1½ inches in diameter. In a medium saucepan, bring the chicken stock to a boil. Add the meatballs and cover. Simmer for 20 minutes. Add noodles if desired, or bok choy *(see khaki suggestion above)*. Continue to simmer until the noodles are done, then serve as soup, adding hot sauce if you want.

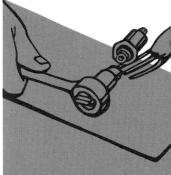

Doctor it up

Tex-Mex balls? Try jalapeño, salsa, and ketchup. Caribbean balls? Ginger, habanero chiles, and honey. Moroccan balls? Cumin, cinnamon, and lamb instead of pork.

What to drink

Shake things up and drink Italian wine with your German meatballs, or sake with the Italian meatballs.

Serve this

Three nights in a row—and not get bored.

serves 2

crouching
tiger, hidder

I first made this dish for the 2001 Oscars, hoping that the flick that inspired it would win. The dish, like the film, is a winner, and I still make it a lot. It's pretty good with a few small potatoes, boiled for about 15 minutes and served hot.

Salt and **pepper**

2 **salmon fillets**, about 8 to 10 ounces each, skin on

2 **leeks**, white and light green parts only, sliced and *then* rinsed thoroughly in a colander

2 tablespoons **unsalted butter**

1 tablespoon **olive oil**

¼ cup **chicken stock** *(page 108)*, canned broth, or water

Juice of 1 **lime**

Sprinkle salt and pepper on the salmon fillets and set aside. In a medium saucepan, cover the leeks with cold water and 2 pinches of salt. Bring to a boil, then drop the heat and simmer for about 15 minutes, or until tender but not mushy. Drain and set aside.

When the leeks are nearly finished, melt the butter with the olive oil in a sauté pan over high heat until it's hot. Place the salmon carefully in the pan, skin-side down, and sear for 2 minutes. Don't touch it during this time, or you'll lose the skin.

salmon

continued

After 2 minutes, use a spatula to carefully loosen the salmon skin from the bottom of the pan, being careful not to tear the skin. Flip the fillets over. Sear for 2 minutes, then loosen again but don't flip. Add the chicken stock and lime juice to the pan, but don't pour it all over the crispy skin. Spread the leeks around the salmon and let simmer for 5 minutes, or until the liquid reduces by half. Taste a leek and adjust the seasonings if necessary.

Serve the salmon, skin-side up, with the leeks hiding it. Get it? Hidden Salmon.

Doctor it up

Oh, what the hell, how about a few slices of bacon crumbled over the top?

Serve this

If this isn't a date dish, I don't know what is. You don't have to call it "Crouching Tiger, Hidden Salmon" if you don't want. I mean, your date might just think you're weird.

What to drink

A sharp, not sweet, German Riesling.

fish stew with beer and chorizo

Occupying the top slot of the food chain means more than getting to eat all the steak you want. The ocean is teeming with tasty critters just begging to be tossed into pots. This stew is perfect for people who think they don't like fish: It's tasty, hearty, filling, and hardly fishy at all. And besides, it's got pork. Can't argue with that.

1   medium **chorizo sausage**, about 1 pound, cut into ½-inch cubes

2   tablespoons **olive oil**

1   medium **Spanish onion**, halved and sliced

1   medium **carrot**, peeled and sliced

2   **garlic cloves**, smashed and minced

2   tablespoons **country-style** *(whole-grain)* **mustard**

¼   cup **ketchup**

1   **bay leaf**

1   cup **bottled clam juice**

1   bottle *(12 ounces)* **medium-amber beer**

3 to 4 cups **water**, or more if needed

1   pound **russet potatoes**, cut into ½-inch cubes *(peeling optional)*

1   can *(14½ ounces)* **white beans**, drained

1   pound **monkfish fillet**, cut into 1-inch chunks

½   pound **red** or **pink snapper**, cut into 1-inch chunks

½   pound **flounder**, cut into 1-inch chunks

Salt and **pepper**

1   bag *(about 5 ounces)* **baby spinach**

continued

In a soup pot over high heat, sauté the chorizo cubes in the olive oil until they brown lightly and release their orangey-spicy oils, about 6 minutes. Using a slotted spoon, transfer the chorizo chunks to a small bowl.

Add the onion and carrot to the pot and sauté until soft. Add the garlic and sauté for 1 minute more. Add the mustard and ketchup. Cook for 1 minute. Add the bay leaf and cook for 1 minute more. Add the clam juice and beer. Scrape up any browned bits from the bottom of the pan and stir to incorporate them into the liquid. Add 3 cups water, bring to a light boil, lower the heat, cover, and let the broth simmer over medium-low heat for 60 minutes. *(If you taste your stock every few minutes or so, you'll really notice the flavor change from minute to minute.)* If your liquid level starts to drop, add more water to make up the difference.

Add the potatoes and simmer for 15 minutes. Add the beans and stir in gently.

Season the fish with salt and pepper. Add the monkfish chunks to stew and simmer for 5 minutes. Add the snapper and flounder chunks and continue to simmer for 5 more minutes, or until all the fish is opaque. Taste the stew for seasoning, adding salt and pepper if necessary.

Add the spinach *(all of it, even if it seems like a lot)* and cover the pot until the spinach is wilted but not overcooked, about 2 minutes. Stir to incorporate into the stew.

Ladle into deep bowls and serve with crusty bread in front of the TV.

Doctor it up

Try different kinds of fish, like cod, halibut, or eel. Also, use bacon instead of chorizo. Yum.

Serve this

On Sunday night before a big week at work. Fish is brain food.

What to drink

Call me redundant, but this stew begs for an awfully cold beer.

chicken thigh and white bean stew (not exactly a cassoulet)

No joke, you can make this dish for under ten bucks, except for the pancetta, but you probably have a little leftover in the fridge anyway. In a pinch, cut up a few slices of bacon, but be careful not to burn it.

½ pound **pancetta** or bacon, cut into ½-inch cubes

Olive oil

8 **chicken thighs**, skin on and bone in

1 medium **onion**, sliced

2 **carrots**, peeled and sliced

2 stalks **celery**, sliced

2 stalks **leeks**, white and light green parts only, sliced and *then* rinsed thoroughly

2 cups **chicken stock** *(page 108)* or canned broth, at room temperature

½ teaspoon **red pepper flakes**

1 teaspoon **dried thyme**

1 teaspoon **dried sage**

1 tablespoon **dry mustard**

1 bunch **collard greens**, tough stems removed and leaves cut into 1-inch strips

Salt and **pepper**

1 can *(about 14½ ounces)* **white beans**, drained

A few shavings of **Parmesan cheese** for garnish

C06 Supper

continued

Preheat the oven to 350°F. In a large enameled Dutch oven or saucepan over medium heat, sauté the pancetta in a drizzle of olive oil until tender but not brown. Remove with a slotted spoon, leaving the drippings behind.

In two batches, sauté the chicken thighs, skin-side down, until well browned, about 6 to 7 minutes. Be careful not to crowd the pan. Turn and sauté on the other side until browned, another 4 minutes. Using tongs or a slotted spoon, transfer the thighs to a plate.

Using a few paper towels wadded up, blot up the excess fat from pot, leaving in about 2 tablespoons. Sauté the onion, carrots, celery, and leeks until the onion is soft and translucent.

Add the chicken stock in a slow stream so as not to cool down the pot too much. Scrape up any browned bits from the bottom of the pan and stir to incorporate them into the liquid. Add the red pepper flakes, dried herbs, and dry mustard and stir in. Add the collard greens and stir to coat. Season to taste with salt and pepper. Stir in the beans. Lay the chicken thighs skin-side up on top of the beans and greens, making sure the browned skin is not submerged. Pour any accumulated juices from the plate holding the chicken over all, then cover and slip into the oven for 45 minutes.

Uncover the pot and, using a vegetable peeler, shave Parmesan cheese over the chicken. Return uncovered dish to the oven and bake, allowing the cheese to brown on the chicken, about 15 minutes more.

Doctor it up

Swap out the bacon and use a nice hard summer sausage, cut into ½-inch cubes, instead.

Serve this

In bowls, on the deadest day of the whole winter.

What to drink

A good Aussie Shiraz. Or if you're feeling rich, a lusty French Syrah.

four-corners chili

I grew up in Colorado, where chili is considered an art. As it should be. Much like barbecue, everyone's chili is slightly different, with variations by region, class, background, everything. This chili is a fairly mild, meat-based chunky one with beef, pork, and lamb, which adds a cool angle. No beans here. If you want beans, serve them on the side, and make them red.

This tastes a hell of a lot better the day *after* you make it. So make it on Saturday and eat it on Sunday. And also for lunch on Monday. Oh, and make sure you taste this recipe frequently along the way. This is a real tinkerer's dish. Taste, adjust, taste, adjust, and repeat.

½ pound **beef stew meat**, cut into 1-inch cubes

½ pound **lamb stew meat**, cut into 1-inch cubes

½ pound **pork stew meat**, cut into 1-inch cubes *(shoulder is best)*

4 to 6 **short ribs** *(optional)*

Salt and **pepper**

3 slices **bacon**, chopped

1 teaspoon **olive oil**

1 large **yellow onion**, diced

2 medium **carrots**, peeled and diced

2 small **jalapeños**, sliced *(If you like a lot of heat, leave the seeds and white pithy stuff. If you want less heat, get rid of them. You can always add heat later.)*

7 **garlic cloves**; 3 smashed and minced, 4 halved

continued

1   tablespoon **dried oregano**

1   tablespoon **dried sage leaves**

1   small can *(about 6 ounces)*
    tomato paste

½   cup **ketchup**

1   bottle *(12 ounces)* of **your
    favorite beer** *(don't use the bad
    stuff . . . if you won't drink it,
    don't cook with it)*

1½ tablespoons **ground cumin** *(keep
    it handy, you may want to add
    more as it cooks)*

¼   cup **chili powder** *(You can use
    a store-bought blend, or you
    can make your own. My current
    favorite is equal parts achiote
    powder, chipotle powder, and
    pimiento de la vera powder.)*

1   tablespoon **ground cinnamon**

1   teaspoon freshly grated **nutmeg**

3   cups **chicken stock** *(page 108)*
    or canned broth, plus more
    if needed

Season the meat with salt and pepper and set aside. Preheat the oven to 300°F.

In a large, ovenproof pot or Dutch oven with a tight-fitting lid, sauté the bacon in the olive oil over high heat until the fat has rendered. Remove the bacon from the pan with a slotted spoon onto a bed of paper towels. Blot up the excess fat from the pot with additional paper towels, leaving in about 2 to 3 table-spoons. Then, working in batches and being careful not to overcrowd the pan *(this is* way *important, 'cause if you pack it all in there, it won't brown)*, sear the beef, lamb, and pork over high heat until browned and crispy on all sides, about 6 minutes total per batch. Using a slotted spoon, transfer to a bowl or plate large enough to catch all the juices.

Blot any excess fat from the pot, leaving about 2 tablespoons. Sauté the onion, carrots, and jalapeños until soft, about 4 minutes. Add the minced garlic, oregano, and sage and sauté for 2 minutes more. Add the tomato paste and ketchup and sauté for 3 to 4 min-utes more, until the tomato begins to deepen in color, turning slightly brown. Add the beer, stirring well to liquefy the tomato, then add the cumin, and chili powder, cinnamon, nutmeg, and garlic halves.

Return the meat and any accumulated juices to the pot, stirring to coat with the chili mix-ture. Add the chicken stock, stirring well. The chili should be fairly wet, with about half the

continued

C06 Supper

139

meat submerged. *(Add more chicken stock if needed.)* Bring to a low simmer, but do not boil. When a low simmer is reached, cover and slide the chili into the oven.

Bake the chili for 2 hours without stirring. After 2 hours, taste and adjust the seasonings. Add more stock if you need it to keep the meat half-submerged. Stir the chili. Reduce the oven temperature to 250°F and bake for 1 hour more.

Sprinkle reserved bacon over the chili. Let the chili cool, then refrigerate overnight. Reheat on the stove top by bringing it to a low simmer and holding it there for 20 minutes. Serve hot.

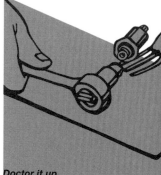

Doctor it up

Throw in some chopped sun-dried tomatoes with the ketchup for yet another level of smokiness.

Serve this

With the cornbread on page 26 or with a big bowl of rice.

What to drink

A dusty California Cab.

beef tenderloin in horseradish crust

Tenderloin has incredible texture—soft, smooth, and, of course, *tender*. But it's not bursting with flavor the way a rib eye or porterhouse is, and it needs a kick. Enter horseradish, beef's best friend.

The key to this recipe is the searing. Make sure your pan is way hot, and when you're searing, don't move the tenderloin around any more than you have to. You *want* all those charred brown bits stuck to the bottom of the pan *("they" call that stuff fond, as in "nice fond under that beef")*. It won't make the pan harder to clean, and besides, you need that *fond* for the crust.

3   large **russet potatoes**, scrubbed and cut into 1-inch slices *(peeling optional)*

1   **beef tenderloin roast**, about 1¼ to 1½ pounds *(make sure you talk your plans over with the butcher to get the best cut)*

5   tablespoons **unsalted butter**

2   teaspoons **olive oil**

¼   cup **wine** or **beer** *(chicken broth will work; use water if you must)*

½   cup **Japanese panko crumbs** *(check your gourmet grocery store, like Whole Foods; bread crumbs will work too)*, plus extra if needed

continued

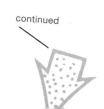

⅓ cup **prepared horseradish** *(you'll know it's prepared because it's in a jar)*

2 **garlic cloves**, smashed and chopped

2 to 3 tablespoons chopped **fresh tarragon** or 2 to 3 teaspoons dried tarragon

2 teaspoons **coarse salt**

A few grindings of **pepper**

Preheat the oven to 450°F. Arrange the potato slices in a shallow roasting pan and set aside. The potatoes will serve as the "rack" for your tenderloin. Using your sharpest knife, trim away any excess fat from your tenderloin. There probably won't be much, and remember, "excess" is in the eye of the beholder.

Melt 1 tablespoon of the butter with the olive oil in a heavy sauté pan until hot but not yet smoking. *(If it starts to smoke, back down the heat slightly and let it cool.)* While the oil is heating, pat the tenderloin dry with paper towels. It should be dry before it hits the pan. Put the tenderloin in the sauté pan and brown on all sides, about 5 to 6 minutes total. Transfer your tenderloin to the roasting pan and let it rest atop the potatoes.

Return the sauté pan to the heat and drizzle in the wine or beer. Scrape up the browned bits from the bottom of the pan. Cook to reduce liquid by half, then remove from the heat.

Meantime, using your hands, mix together the panko crumbs, horseradish, garlic, tarragon, salt, and pepper in a medium bowl. Drizzle the sauce from the sauté pan over the mixture and toss until all the ingredients are evenly distributed and the crumbs begin to clump together. If mixture is too wet, add more panko crumbs.

Rub the crust mixture over the entire tenderloin, patting it down to adhere. The mixture should form a layer over the entire piece of meat. Replace the meat on top of the potatoes.

Slide the roasting pan into the oven. Roast for 5 minutes, then reduce the oven temperature to 400°F. Roast for an additional 20 to 25 minutes. The crust should be browned and just crispy. Use an instant-read thermometer to check the internal temperature for doneness—it should hit 125°F for rare, 130°F for medium-rare. Any hotter than that and you'll need extra mayo on the sandwiches tomorrow.

Remove the tenderloin from the oven and transfer to a cutting board. Let stand for 10 minutes before slicing, to let the juices redistribute themselves *(you know the feeling)*. Test the potatoes with a fork. If not yet tender, slide back into the oven while the tenderloin rests.

Slice the tenderloin on the diagonal into four 1½-inch slices and serve with a pat of butter on top of each slice. Spoon the potatoes alongside and eat.

Doctor it up

Go somewhere else with the crust. Skip the horseradish and use a head or two of roasted garlic, or chop up a whole bunch of fresh rosemary, thyme, sage, or any other herb or spice. Cumin is good. So is cracked black pepper. Dry mustard. Gremolata *(parsley, lemon, and garlic, pounded in a mortar and pestle)*. Chile powder. Need I go on?

Serve this

With that great bottle of wine your boss gave you this year instead of a bonus. Toast the bastard or biatch anyway.

What to drink

See above. If you have to buy your own bottle, get a nice hearty California Cabernet. Or hang the wine and mix yourself a martini. That's what I'd probably do.

baked ziti with

If you're lactose-intolerant or don't eat dairy, walk on by this recipe, 'cause this one is all about the cheese. Five kinds, in ample quantities. What more could you want? Oh yeah, meatballs. Use the ones on page 125, and start with them uncooked.

FOR THE **SAUCE**

3   tablespoons **olive oil**

2   tablespoons **dried oregano**

1 to 2 teaspoons **garlic powder** *(not garlic salt)*

2   tablespoons **dried minced onion**

1   small can *(about 6 ounces)* **tomato paste**

1   can *(about 14½ ounces)* **diced tomatoes** *(imported Italian are best)*, with their juice

2   tablespoons **balsamic vinegar**

½   cup **chicken stock** *(page 108)* or canned broth

1   pound **dried ziti**

10 to 12 **meatballs**

1   cup shredded **Asiago cheese**

½   cup shredded **provolone cheese**

¼   cup **ricotta cheese**

1   cup shredded **mozzarella cheese**

½   cup grated **Parmesan cheese**, preferably Parmigiano-Reggiano

meatballs

Bring a large pot full of salted water to a boil over high heat.

make the sauce

In a medium saucepan, heat up the olive oil, oregano, garlic powder, and dried onion. Cook for 1 minute, then add the tomato paste. Stir to incorporate, then add the diced tomatoes and juice, vinegar, and chicken stock. Stir and let simmer over low heat, covered, for 30 minutes.

Preheat the oven to 375°F. Add the pasta to the boiling water and cook until just undercooked, shaving about 2 minutes off the package directions. Drain, then empty into a baking dish. Stir in the sauce. Add the meatballs to the pasta, distributing them evenly. Add the Asiago, provolone, ricotta, and mozzarella cheeses, stirring to just barely incorporate cheeses into the pasta. Sprinkle the Parmesan on top. Bake for 20 minutes, until the cheeses are browned and bubbly on top.

Doctor it up

Heat up your sauce with some red pepper flakes. Or, if you don't have meatballs, substitute Italian sausages that you've chopped into meatball-size chunks.

Serve this

The day after you've made extra meatballs.

What to drink

Italian table wine.

C06 Supper

pasta with

and bacon

shrimp

Everyone loves pasta. Everyone loves shrimp. Everyone loves bacon. What more do you want? This is a great summer pasta because it's satisfying, but light in flavor. Which also makes it a great pasta to serve on a third date. It'll fuel you up, but not weigh you down.

Salt

1 pound medium **shrimp**, uncooked

½ pound **slab bacon**, diced, or 4 slices bacon, snipped into pieces with scissors

2 tablespoons **olive oil**, plus more for drizzling

½ pound dried **linguine** or **spaghetti**

¼ cup **white wine** *(use a decent white, an Italian Pinot Grigio, one that you'll drink with dinner)*

2 **garlic cloves**, smashed and diced

A few **red pepper flakes**, finely crushed *(optional)*

A couple handfuls **arugula leaves** *(about 2 to 3 ounces)*, chopped

Zest and juice of 1 **lemon**

½ cup grated **Parmesan cheese**

Fill your largest pot with water and set it on high. Throw in a handful of salt, more than you think you need. Cover it and bring it to a boil. This could take 20 minutes, so get this going before you pour yourself a drink.

Pour the drink and prepare the shrimp: Peel and devein the shrimp by slicing straight down the back with your paring knife and scraping out that black intestine. *(You don't have to do this, because it won't kill you to eat it, but most people don't dig the veins.)* Set them aside in a small bowl with a few cubes of ice on top.

continued

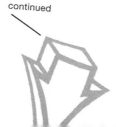

Put the bacon in a large sauté pan over medium-high heat. Drizzle it with a little olive oil and sauté it until most of the fat has rendered and the bacon becomes crispy. Remove from the heat until your water boils and you put your linguine in.

Once the linguine is cooking *(it should take about 10 to 12 minutes, but don't take my word for it, check your package)*, return the sauté pan to medium-high heat and add the 2 tablespoons olive oil, the wine, garlic, and red pepper flakes. Add the shrimp in a single layer. Sauté for 2 minutes, then turn the shrimp and sauté for 2 minutes more. Reduce the heat to low. Lay the arugula over the top of the shrimp.

Drain the pasta, then add to the pan, covering the arugula. Mix thoroughly, coating all the pasta and adding more olive oil if necessary. Add the lemon zest and juice and mix. Add the Parmesan. Remove from the heat and serve immediately, with one last drizzle of olive oil *(at this point in the preparation, use the good stuff if you've got it)*.

Doctor it up

If they look good at the store, throw in a handful of grape or cherry tomatoes alongside the shrimp while they're sautéing. You could also throw in some basil instead of that arugula, or maybe some olives that you've sliced in half. Maybe some anchovy fillets. Or some zucchini shavings. Or an artichoke heart. Okay, enough already.

Serve this

During the summer, when you don't feel hungry, but you are.

What to drink

An Italian white, whatever you used in the recipe.

soppressata sandwich panzanella

Desperation is the other mother of invention. This recipe came during an ugly post-oral-surgery fit of hunger: It was late, my mouth hurt, and the only thing in the fridge was a leftover crusty-breaded soppressata hero. Lightbulb: panzanella, even better than the sandwich it started out as. I like soppressata, but you should mix and match any toppings you want–prosciutto, mortadella, roasted peppers, onions, cheeses, whatever.

1 **sandwich** from your favorite Italian deli

1 large, ripe **tomato**, cubed *(in season)*, or 1 can *(about 14 ounces)* diced tomatoes *(don't buy crappy fresh tomatoes)*

2 tablespoons **olive oil**

1 tablespoon **balsamic vinegar**

Salt and **pepper**

Red pepper flakes to taste *(optional)*

A few gratings of **lemon zest**

Press unwrapped sandwich under a cast-iron pan for 30 minutes. Using a serrated knife, cube the sandwich into bite-size pieces and toss into a medium bowl. Add the remaining ingredients and combine well. Cover and refrigerate for at least 1 hour, stirring twice and adding more olive oil if necessary to keep bread moist. Bring to room temperature before serving.

Doctor it up

Don't have a sandwich handy? Make cold pizza panzanella instead. Same principle, only you don't have to press it as long.

Serve this

To yourself, solo.

What to drink

Chianti, Montepulciano, or any friendly Italian red.

red wine

If you haven't sealed the deal yet, this dish, executed well, will signal the end of negotiations. It's a do-or-die dish and it demands a response, one way or the other. Good thing it's easy. The key to this one is using the best ingredients, and that'll mean a visit to the best gourmet food store you can find. This might mean a drive, not to mention an expensive bill, but hey, are you in it to win it or what? Practice this one once or twice before serving it to someone else . . . not because it's difficult, but just so you're familiar with the pacing. Don't use regular white rice for risotto. It won't work and you'll look like an ass. Get the good stuff *(Arborio or a similar sturdy rice)* at the gourmet shop, and ask the person there for help if you need it. No shame in accepting an assist at the grocery store.

4 cups **chicken stock** *(page 108)* or canned broth

4 ounces **pancetta**, chopped into ½-inch chunks

1 medium **onion**

2 teaspoons **olive oil**

2 **anchovy fillets** *(Even if you hate anchovies, add them anyway. I promise you won't taste them.)*

1 **garlic clove**, smashed and minced

1 teaspoon **Dijon mustard**

1 teaspoon **dried sage leaves**

2 cups **Arborio rice**

1 glass *(about ¾ cup)* good **Italian red wine**, like Chianti or Sangiovese

½ cup grated **Romano cheese**

A few fresh **sage leaves**

Zest of 1 **lemon**

risotto

Put the chicken stock in a medium saucepan on the back burner, over medium heat. You want it to be, and stay, warm while you're cooking your risotto. Don't boil it, just heat it up to a simmer.

In a large saucepan or Dutch oven, sauté the pancetta and onion in the olive oil until the bacon is crispy, about 6 minutes. Add the anchovies, breaking them up with a wooden spoon. Add the garlic, mustard, and dried sage and stir.

Add the rice to the pan. Stir to coat with the bacon and onion mixture. Cook for 1 minute, then add the wine. Stir. Next, add 2 ladlefuls of the hot chicken stock. Stir for a couple of minutes as the liquid begins to be absorbed by the rice. When most of the liquid is absorbed, add another ladleful of stock and stir. Keep adding stock as it evaporates. The key is to keep the risotto wet but not submerged, cooking but not burning. Keep your eye on it.

Taste the risotto as you go. When it's just barely still crunchy on the inside, but nice and soft and silky on the outside, add the cheese and stir through. You're in business. Spoon into bowls, tearing the sage leaves and sprinkling the lemon zest over the top.

Doctor it up

Put a poached egg on top for kicks, and really good flavor. Or, if it's summer, use white wine instead of red and ditch the sage for peas and mint.

Serve this

To a date. Here's a tip: If you don't want to be sweating over the stove for 20 minutes while your guest sits aimlessly, you can cook this risotto almost all the way, like 15 minutes maybe, to the just-barely too crunchy stage. Only use three-quarters of the liquid, then slide the risotto to the back burner to rest until you're ready for dinner. Finish it off by returning it to the heat and stirring through the last of the stock, just 5 minutes or so. Add the cheese and lemon and you're done.

What to drink

Drink whatever you're cooking with.

It's raining. Or snowing. You picked up *Kill Bill 2* at the DVD store on sale for $6.99. There's a rotisserie chicken in the fridge *(or the leftover chicken from the stock you made)*. There's beer in there, too. You've got a few frozen peas in the freezer? And some frozen crusts? Looks like a chicken pot pie night. This one has a crust on the bottom as well as the top. Which is good news if you ask me. This recipe calls for frozen pie crusts, but if you'd rather make your own, go for it.

2   frozen 9-inch **pie crusts**

2   tablespoons **olive oil**

4   slices **bacon**, snipped into
    small pieces

1   small **onion**, sliced

2   medium **carrots**, peeled and
    sliced

2   stalks **celery**, sliced

2   **garlic cloves**, sliced

2   tablespoons **dried mushrooms**,
    minced

¼   cup **country-style** *(whole-grain)*
    mustard

2   teaspoons smooth **Dijon
    mustard**

2   tablespoons **red wine vinegar**

1   tablespoon **all-purpose flour**

2   cups **cooked chicken meat**,
    torn into bite-size pieces

½   cup **chicken stock** *(page 108)*
    or canned broth

1   bottle *(12 ounces)* **full-bodied
    beer**

serves 6

beer and mustard

Preheat the oven to 350°F. Remove both pie crusts from the freezer. Set 1 pie crust aside to thaw slightly. Prick the other crust with a fork several times on the bottom, being careful not to pierce the foil pan. On the center rack of the oven, bake the pricked pie crust for 6 to 8 minutes, until it just begins to brown. Watch it carefully, and don't let it go too long. When it is golden, remove it and set it aside.

In a large saucepan, sauté the olive oil, bacon, onion, carrots, and celery until the bacon is crispy, about 5 minutes. Add the garlic and sauté for 1 minute more. Stir in the mushrooms, mustards, and vinegar. Add the flour and, using a whisk, incorporate until there are no lumps. Add the chicken meat. Stir to coat. Add the chicken stock and beer. Cover and simmer for 5 minutes. Remove from the heat.

When the filling has cooled slightly, spoon it into the baked pie crust. Drape the other crust over the top, then press at the edges to seal, folding over if necessary. Make a few slits in the top of the pie. Bake for 20 to 25 minutes, or until the top crust is golden brown.

Doctor it up

Howsabout a pork pot pie? Maybe duck? Mmm, turkey. And if you really must, bake this in an ovenproof dish with just one crust on top. It still rocks.

Serve this

Hot. And serve it again the next day after it's been refrigerated, then reheated at 350°F for 15 minutes.

What to drink

A bottle of the same beer you cooked this with.

chicken pot pie

makes 2 loins, one for 2 of you to eat tonight and one for sandwiches later on

tequila

Pork. One of God's greatest creations, truly. There is very little on the savory side of life that isn't improved with a little pork. But while my heart belongs to bacon, I'll always have a place in there for a perfectly roasted pork loin. This is one way to do it. Work closely with your butcher on this; tell him you want the best he's got. Oh, and make two, because a pork loin sandwich on sourdough with mustard and orange marmalade is a sublime experience.

2 **pork tenderloins**, about 2 pounds total

½ cup **tequila**

¼ cup **olive oil**, plus 2 teaspoons

3 **garlic cloves**, smashed

2 medium **onions**, peeled and quartered

1 **jalapeño chile**, sliced

2 small **limes**, rolled *(on the countertop to stir up the juices)* and quartered

¼ cup **coarse salt** *(this will seem like a lot, but you need it)*

A few grindings of **pepper**

½ cup **apricot jam** or jelly

2 tablespoons **fresh rosemary**, coarsely chopped

pork loin

Start by marinating the tenderloins: Slice a 1-inch-deep slit *(about halfway through the tenderloin)* down the length of each tenderloin. Place the tenderloins in a large Ziploc bag. Add the tequila, ¼ cup olive oil, garlic, onions, jalapeño, lime quarters, salt, and pepper, pressing the marinade into the slits. Refrigerate for at least 2 hours, or overnight.

Preheat the oven to 450°F. In a large, oven-proof frying pan over very high heat, warm up the 2 teaspoons olive oil and brown the pork loins on 2 sides. Remove from the heat. Spoon the apricot jam into the slits in the tenderloins, half of the jam in each. Reposition them in the skillet, cut-side down. Slide into the oven, reduce the oven temperature to 350°F, and roast for 10 minutes. Sprinkle chopped rosemary over the top, rotate the pan 180°, and roast for 10 minutes more.

Remove the pork and cover with a piece of aluminum foil, "tenting" it. Let rest for 15 minutes before slicing, crosswise on the diagonal.

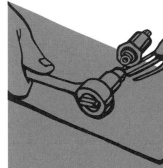

Doctor it up

Not into tequila? Try wine. Or port. Or bourbon. Or gin. Yum, gin. Also, cut a few potatoes into 1-inch chunks and put them in alongside the pork. They'll be done at the same time.

Serve this

With couscous, which is the easiest thing ever to make. It's literally just add water. Check the package.

What to drink

Shots while you're cooking, then an Oregon Pinot Noir with dinner.

surf 'n

Picture it: Long summer night, warm breeze, a few good friends, a whole bucket of ice-cold beer, and a massive pan of warm, spicy, saffrony paella. Sounds good, yeah? Now, add a steak. This looks like a lot of ingredients, but it actually comes together pretty quickly. Just have everything ready before you start. *(Remember, page 10, mise en place?)*

1½ pounds medium **shrimp**

2 tablespoons **olive oil**

4 **chicken thighs**

4 **chicken drumsticks**

4 **Cajun sausages**, about 1½ pounds total, halved cross-wise *(you can also use Italian sausages, hot or sweet)*

3 **anchovy fillets**

1 medium **onion**, diced

2 stalks **celery**, diced

1 medium **bell pepper**, seeded and diced

3 **garlic cloves**, smashed and diced

½ teaspoon **red pepper flakes**, or to taste

2 tablespoons **paprika**

1 **bay leaf**

1 cup **white wine**

2 pinches **saffron threads**

2 cups **Arborio rice**

4 cups **chicken stock** *(page 108)* or canned broth, at room temperature

1 teaspoon **sugar**

Salt and **pepper**

2 tablespoons **unsalted butter**

1 **skirt steak**, 1 to 1½ pounds

Preheat the oven to 325°F. Peel the shrimp and devein them by slicing straight down the back with your paring knife and scraping out that black intestine. *(You don't have to do this, because it won't kill you to eat it, but most people don't dig the veins. If you're alone, it's up to you.)* Put the shrimp in a bowl, cover, and stick them in the fridge for now. Drop the casings into a small saucepan and cover with 2 cups water. Set to a low simmer for stock.

turf paella

In a large Dutch oven or ovenproof sauté pan, warm the olive oil over high heat, then add the chicken pieces, skin-side down, and brown for 6 to 7 minutes on the first side, then turn and brown the other side for another 4 to 5 minutes. Using tongs, transfer to a plate and cover loosely with aluminum foil. Blot up the excess chicken fat from the pot with a wad of paper towels, leaving about 2 tablespoons of fat.

Ditto with the sausages: Sear them on both sides and the cut ends, about 3 minutes per side, or until browned and crispy. Transfer to the same plate as the chicken and blot the fat to leave about 2 tablespoons.

In the same pot, over medium-high heat now, sauté the anchovies, onion, celery, bell pepper, and garlic until soft and fragrant. Pour any accumulated juices from the plate holding the chicken and sausages into the pot. Add the red pepper flakes, paprika, and bay leaf.

Combine the wine and 1 pinch of saffron in a glass and stir with a fork to dissolve. Add the rice to the pot, using a wooden spoon to coat it with onion mixture. Add the saffron wine to the pot and stir to distribute. Scrape up the browned bits from the bottom of the pot, stirring to incorporate them into your rice.

continued

Stir the chicken and sausage pieces into the rice. Strain the shrimp stock and discard the peels. Pour the stock over the rice, then add the chicken stock to just barely cover rice *(it might not require all 4 cups)*. Return the mixture to a boil, then slide the pot into the oven, uncovered. Bake until the rice is just barely done, about 40 minutes. Check halfway through and add more stock if necessary.

Remove the paella from oven, and stir lightly to fluff the rice. Cover loosely to keep warm.

Remove the shrimp from the refrigerator. Do not rinse them. Stir in the sugar, the remaining 1 pinch saffron, and a pinch of salt. In a medium sauté pan over high heat, warm the butter until bubbling but not yet brown. Sauté the shrimp until just cooked, about 1 minute per side. Pour the shrimp and butter over the top of the paella, reserving the butter-coated pan.

Sprinkle the steak with salt and pepper on both sides. Heat up the same medium sauté pan until very hot. Lay the steak in the pan, sear for 3 to 4 minutes on each side until well browned but pink on the inside, then transfer to a cutting board. Let rest for 5 minutes. Slice the steak into thin *(¼-inch)* strips, carving against the grain. Lay over the top of the paella. Serve immediately, directly from the pot.

Doctor it up

Get medieval and add crayfish, clams, octopus, or squid.

Serve this

When it's your turn to host the party for once.

What to drink

As envisioned, ample cold beer. Also, sangria's always fun, and it tends to get people in the hot tub.

six easy vegetables

Face it, you need your veggies. Here's how to cook some of the classics, all easy enough to do alongside any of the suppers in this book. Note: Although I've kept these preparations pretty basic, keep in mind that all vegetables are improved considerably with the addition of bacon pieces and/or the use of bacon fat while cooking. Same goes for mustard, which is an awesome condiment for almost all vegetables.

broccoli

1 head **broccoli**

½ cup **chicken stock** *(page 108)* or canned chicken broth or vegetable broth

Salt and **pepper**

Olive oil for drizzling

Cut the broccoli into florets, leaving as much of the stem as you like. In a medium saucepan fitted with a folding metal steamer, bring the chicken stock to a boil. Place the broccoli into the steamer, salt lightly, and cover tightly. Steam for 6 minutes, or just until tender when pierced with a knife. Sprinkle with salt and pepper and drizzle with olive oil. Done. You can also cook cauliflower the exact same way.

roasted cauliflower

1 head **cauliflower**

Salt and **pepper**

Olive oil for drizzling

Preheat the oven to 425°F. Cut the cauliflower into florets and arrange on a baking sheet. Sprinkle with salt and pepper and drizzle with olive oil. Roast, turning once, just until tender when pierced with a knife, for 15 to 20 minutes. The cauliflower will brown lightly. Serve hot. You can also make broccoli the exact same way.

continued

C06 Supper

microwave spinach

3

1 bag *(about 5 ounces)* **baby spinach**

1 tablespoon **unsalted butter**, at room temperature

1 teaspoon **olive oil**

Salt and **pepper**

Poke 3 holes in the spinach bag. Microwave on high for 1 minute, until wilted. Place the butter in the bottom of a serving bowl. Tear open the bag, empty the spinach into bowl, and drizzle the olive oil over the top. Add salt and pepper to taste and toss with tongs. Eat immediately.

(If you don't want to use the whole bag, put however much you want on a microwave-safe plate. Flip another plate on top of it, upside down. Microwave for 1 minute, then check. Hit it for another minute if you need to. Sprinkle with salt and pepper and drizzle with olive oil. Done.)

braised swiss chard

4

½ bunch **Swiss chard**, any color

2 slices **bacon**, snipped into small pieces *(optional)*

2 teaspoons **olive oil**

¼ cup **chicken stock** *(page 108)* or canned chicken or vegetable broth, or water *(Or beer. Some kind of liquid.)*

Cut off the stalks of the chard and chop coarsely. Tear the leaves in fourths. In a medium sauté pan over medium-high heat, sauté the bacon (if using) until the fat has rendered. Add the olive oil and chopped chard stalks and sauté for 5 minutes, until soft. Add the leaves, using tongs to turn them and coat them. Add the chicken stock and cover partially with a lid. Cook for 15 minutes longer, or until the leaves are tender, then serve. The bacon in this recipe is not crispy, it's more soft and chewy. Different, but I like it.

roasted root vegetables

1   large **turnip**, peeled

2   **parsnips**, peeled

1   large **carrot**, peeled

1   **garlic head**, separated into
    cloves and peeled

Olive oil for drizzling

Salt and **pepper**

Preheat the oven to 400°F. Slice the vegetables into bite-size pieces. Arrange a baking sheet and drizzle with olive oil. Roast for 20 to 25 minutes, until the vegetables are tender. Salt and pepper them while they're still hot. You can also roast radicchio the same way.

sautéed green beans

1   **garlic clove**, minced

2   tablespoons **olive oil**

2   handfuls **frozen green beans**,
    defrosted in the microwave for
    30 seconds *(Buy the beans in a
    bag, not a box. Otherwise, you'll
    be stuck defrosting the whole box
    and you'll have too many beans,
    and who wants that?)*

Salt and **pepper**

In a medium sauté pan over medium-high, sauté the garlic in the olive oil until the oil is hot. Toss in the green beans, watching out for splatter. Add salt and pepper to taste. Sauté for 4 minutes or just until the beans are tender. Done. *(Add a handful of slivered almonds if you're in the mood.)*

07

des

and **now** for the good part.

There are some foodies out there who turn their noses up at sweets. The savory side of life, they contend, is sophisticated, complex, and refined, whereas sweets are, well, sugary and fattening and childish. And besides, they rot your teeth.

They know who they are, and they can kiss my cake. Because dessert is every bit as important as any other part of the meal. It's a trophy. Like a dog who's just rolled over for a treat, you've just rolled through another day, and for better or worse, you deserve a reward for it. Ergo, dessert.

Dessert isn't just an essential part of supper, it's an essential part of the day. It's not to be ignored. So, don't.

And because there's been so much confusion on this point of late, let me say emphatically, once and for all, that fruit and cheese does *not* count as dessert. Period.

sert.

hot fudge
salsa

makes about **2** cups, enough for **4** sundaes

The simplest, and sometimes best, dessert you can make is ice cream with toppings. This chocolate salsa, chunky and rich, borders on being chocolate overload, which is why I like to cut it with a little shot of chile. Gives it an edge, but doesn't overload it with heat.

4 tablespoons *(½ stick)* **butter**

½ cup **cocoa powder**

½ cup **sugar**

¾ cup **sweetened condensed milk**

4 ounces **semisweet chocolate**

½ teaspoon **chile powder**

½ cup chopped **dried cherries**

Your favorite **gourmet chocolate bar** *(about 4 ounces, but who's counting?)*, frozen and smashed into pieces

Handful of **red Spanish peanuts**

In a saucepan over medium heat, melt the butter. Whisk in the cocoa powder and sugar, stirring until dissolved. Add the sweetened condensed milk and whisk until smooth. Simmer for 2 minutes, then remove from the heat and whisk in the semisweet chocolate until smooth.

Pour into a bowl to cool slightly. Add the chile powder, cherries, frozen chocolate bar, and peanuts, then spoon over ice cream. Serve with "chips": crispy butter cookies.

Doctor it up

Booze it up with some kirsch or orange liqueur. And go wild with your ice cream flavor selection: I recently had it on this lime ice cream *(not sorbet)* that I found on the Lower East Side. So good.

Serve this

After a steak.

What to drink

The last glass of wine.

serves **2**

fried cake
with bananas
sugar

One basic rule of good eating is this: If you *can* fry it in butter, you might as well go ahead and do it. It's an immutable fact that whatever "it" is will taste better. I've proven and reproven this axiom, exhaustively, across the food spectrum. Carry on the noble work and prove it yourself with this cake—a French-toast-ish take-off on the best dessert the Big Easy ever produced, Bananas Foster.

4 tablespoons *(½ stick)* **unsalted butter** *(be prepared to use more if you're in the mood)*

Four 1-inch-thick slices of store-bought **pound cake**

1 cup firmly packed **brown sugar**

2 teaspoons **pure vanilla extract**

2 to 3 medium **bananas**, peeled and sliced in half lengthwise, then halved again crosswise

Vanilla ice cream for serving

Over medium-high heat, melt 2 tablespoons of the butter in a large sauté pan. When it's hot but not yet brown, add the pound-cake slices to the pan. Sauté until lightly browned on both sides and crispy around the edges. *(You may have to do this in two shifts, depending on the size of your pan. Just add more butter if you need it, and keep an eye on the heat. Don't burn the butter.)* Transfer the slices to a plate. Keep warm in a low (200°F) oven.

and brown

continued

Add 2 tablespoons butter to the pan. It'll seem like a lot of butter, which is a good thing. Melt it down, then stir in the brown sugar and vanilla, allowing the sugar to dissolve slightly. Add the bananas, using a spoon to coat them with the butter and sugar mixture. Turn the heat down to low and sauté the bananas until soft, about 5 minutes. Remove from the heat.

Lay 2 slices of cake in the bottom of each of 2 bowls, top with a scoop or two of ice cream, and spoon the hot bananas and butter mixture over the top.

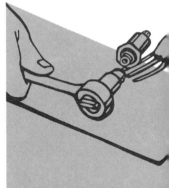

Doctor it up

Throw ½ cup of your favorite rum in with your bananas, and let everything bubble away an extra minute or two. Also, jack up the ice cream element with Ben & Jerry's Phish Food or Häagen Dazs' coffee flavor.

Serve this

When family members come to visit.

What to drink

Irish coffee (1 cup coffee, and 1 shot whiskey, with sugar and heavy cream or half-and-half to taste).

makes about 20 brownies

chocolate-cherry brownies

Brownies go fast, faster than almost any other dessert you can think of. Especially these. The big dark secret? Brown sugar. Although it doesn't really make them more chocolate-y, it makes them, well, fudgier. And after all, fudginess is what we all want in a brownie, isn't it?

Cooking spray for the pan

4 ounces **bitter** or **semisweet chocolate**, coarsely chopped *(in a pinch, you can use chocolate chips)*

4 tablespoons *(½ stick)* **unsalted butter**

Pinch of **salt**

1½ cups **granulated sugar**

½ cup firmly packed **brown sugar**

3 **whole eggs** plus 2 **egg yolks**, lightly beaten *(make a quick omelet with the leftover whites, or choke 'em down Rocky-style, or just throw them away)*

1 tablespoon **pure vanilla extract**

1 cup **all-purpose flour**

2 tablespoons **cocoa powder**

1 cup chopped **nuts** *(pecans, walnuts, hazelnuts, whatever)*

½ cup **dried cherries**, finely chopped

Preheat the oven to 350°F. Line a 9-by-13-inch baking pan with aluminum foil or parchment *(baking)* paper, then spray lightly with the cooking spray. In a microwave-safe bowl or coffee mug, zap the chocolate and butter for 1 minute. Stir, then hit it for another 30 seconds if you need to. The chocolate should be completely melted, but not bubbling. Pour into a large mixing bowl and let cool.

When the chocolate mixture has cooled, add the salt and sugars. Mix well, then add the eggs, yolks, and vanilla. Mix just until incorporated, then add the flour and cocoa powder. Finally, fold in the nuts and cherries.

Scrape the batter into your prepared pan, smooth it out, and bake for about 25 minutes, or until the center of the brownies is firm to the touch. They should feel slightly underdone, though firm to the touch, with the beginning of a crust on top. Let cool in pan on a wire rack for 30 minutes, then cut into squares and serve from pan.

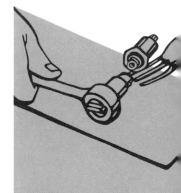

Doctor it up

Lose the cherries; spread a cup of sweetened flaked coconut on a baking sheet. Toast at 300°F for about 10 minutes, or until golden *(watch carefully so you don't burn it)*. Mix this in when you're adding the nuts. Or, add peanut butter: When you've spread the batter out in the pan, dot with creamy or crunchy peanut butter. *(You'll need extra milk when eating this variation.)*

Serve this

When you want to see people's eyes cross.

What to drink

A big glass of milk.

butterscotch chew bread

It's time to blow the lid off of the chew-bread secret. Because if you didn't grow up in the South *(which I didn't)*, you likely haven't heard about it. I first heard about chew bread in *Gourmet* magazine's letters section, in a letter from someone named Gale. I made it that night, and I've made variations on it about a billion times since then, changing it up each time. This is my favorite version. It's pretty funny calling it bread, considering it's nothing but dessert, but hey, I just work here.

Cooking spray for the pan

½ cup *(1 stick)* **unsalted butter**

1 pound **light brown sugar**

2 cups **all-purpose flour**

½ teaspoon **baking powder**

4 large **eggs**

3 teaspoons **pure vanilla extract**

½ cup **almonds**, chopped

12 ounces **butterscotch chips**

Preheat the oven to 350°F. Lightly spray a 9-by-13-inch pan with the cooking spray. Rip off a piece of wax paper and line the bottom of your pan with it, pressing it down then turning it over so both sides are greased.

In a microwave-safe bowl, zap the butter for 1 minute. Remove and stir. Hit it again for another 20 seconds if you need to, until it's melted but not bubbling. Let it cool.

C07 Dessert

continued

Using a whisk, combine the brown sugar, flour, and baking powder in a large bowl.

Ditch the whisk for a wooden spoon and beat in the eggs one at a time. Beat in the melted butter and the vanilla. Fold in the almonds and butterscotch chips. Pour the batter into the prepared pan.

Bake for 40 minutes, or until a wooden toothpick inserted into the middle comes out clean, with no uncooked goo in it. Let cool in the pan on a wire rack. Cut into squares and eat.

Doctor it up

Some subs for the nuts and butter-scotch that I've tried: pecans, walnuts, macadamia nuts, peanuts, coconut, chopped dried fruits, crumbled maple sugar, chocolate chips, white chocolate, chopped Reese's peanut butter cups . . . and so on . . .

Serve this

At, or between, any and all meals.

What to drink

Great on a coffee break, or just back it with a glass of water.

There's a bakery outside my window where people line up for cupcakes. Frankly, I'd rather have a really good cookie. They're way tastier, much easier to eat, and they don't make you feel like you're at an office party to celebrate some dude in accounting's birthday. In my kitchen, cookies are the new cupcake. Besides, they're easier to make.

FOR THE **COOKIE BASE**

1 cup *(2 sticks)* **unsalted butter**, at room temperature

½ cup **granulated sugar**

1 cup firmly packed **brown sugar**

2 teaspoons **pure vanilla extract**

2 **eggs**

2 cups **all-purpose flour**

1 teaspoon **salt**

1 teaspoon **baking soda**

FOR **CHOCOLATE CHIP COOKIES:**

¼ cup **all-purpose flour**

12 ounces **semisweet chocolate chips**

FOR **OATMEAL COOKIES:**

2 cups **old-fashioned rolled oats**

1 teaspoon **ground cinnamon**

FOR **PEANUT BUTTER COOKIES:**

¼ cup **all-purpose flour**

¼ cup **smooth peanut butter**

12 ounces **peanut butter bits**

cookie tl

make the cookie base

Preheat the oven to 350°F. In a large bowl, beat together the butter and sugars until creamy, about 3 minutes with an electric mixer or about 4 to 5 minutes by hand. Add the vanilla and eggs and mix well. In another small bowl, whisk together the flour, salt, and baking soda. Add the flour mixture to the butter and sugar mixture, stirring until just combined. Don't overbeat it or your cookies will be gummy.

Add your flavor combination, mixing until just barely incorporated. Plop in 1 to 2 heaping spoonful mounds onto a baking sheet lined with parchment *(baking)* paper, 2 to 4 inches apart, depending on how big you're going. Bake only 1 sheet at a time, using the center rack in your oven. Bake for 9 to 11 minutes, or even longer for big mounds, until golden brown. Let cool on the baking sheets for a few minutes, then transfer to wire racks.

Doctor it up

Make any of these as bars rather than cookies. Just jack the oven up to 375°F and bake in a greased 9-by-13-inch pan for about 20 to 25 minutes. You'll save all kinds of time.

Serve this

Constantly, until the batch is gone. Then make more.

What to drink

More milk please.

makes 2 or 3 dozen cookies, depending on how big you go

ree-way

chocolate cake with white frosting (a great birthday cake)

makes one **9**-inch double-layer cake

This is the chocolate cake that my grandfather, who is the best cook I ever met, used to make when I would visit in the summers. Actually, truth be told, I'm sure my grandmother made it more often than Gramp did. Whatever, it's a great cake. Make it at least a half-day before you plan to serve it, because it needs to cool for about 2 hours before you should even think about frosting it.

Cooking spray and **flour** for the pans

FOR THE **CAKE**

2 cups **all-purpose flour**

1 cup **granulated sugar**

1 cup **unsweetened cocoa powder**

2 teaspoons **baking soda**

½ teaspoon **salt**

2 large **eggs**, at room temperature

2 teaspoons **pure vanilla extract**

½ cup **vegetable oil**

¾ cup **buttermilk**

2 tablespoons **white vinegar**

1 cup **boiling water**

FOR THE **FROSTING**

1 box *(1 pound)* **powdered sugar**

2 tablespoons **unsalted butter,** at room temperature

1 teaspoon **pure vanilla extract**

3 to 4 tablespoons **whole** or **evaporated milk**

Preheat the oven to 350°F. Lightly spray cooking spray into two 9-inch round cake pans. Knock a little flour around in it and tap out the excess. Cut 2 rounds of parchment *(baking)* paper by placing the pan on top of the paper and running a knife around the perimeter to cut out a circle. Place each parchment circle into each sprayed pan, first spraying both sides with cooking spray.

continued

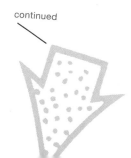

make the cake

Sift together the flour, granulated sugar, cocoa powder, baking soda, and salt by tapping it through a sieve into a large bowl. In a separate bowl, whisk together the eggs, vanilla, oil, and buttermilk. Make a small well in the dry ingredients. Fill the well with the egg mixture. Using a wooden spoon, stir gently and slowly to incorporate the egg mixture. Add the vinegar and mix well. Add the boiling water and stir well.

Divide the batter evenly between the prepared cake pans. Bake for 20 to 25 minutes, or until the cake starts to come away from the sides of the pan and a toothpick stuck into the middle of the cake comes out relatively clean. Let cool in the pans on wire racks for 15 minutes, then turn them out onto the wire racks to cool completely, about 2 hours.

make the frosting

Beat together the powdered sugar, butter, and vanilla. Add the milk until you get the consistency you want: spreadable, but not runny.

Put one layer on a cake plate, top-side down. Frost the top liberally. Place the other cake on top, top-side up, and give it a press. Spread frosting across the top and on all sides of the cake, smoothing as you go. Do this gently, or your cake will be torn to pieces.

Doctor it up

Spread a thin layer of raspberry jam on to each cake layer while it's still cooling. Frost over the top. You can make this as a 9-by-13-inch sheet cake, too. Just bake it a little bit longer.

Serve this

On a birthday. Hers, his, or your own. If you make them a birthday cake, they'll never, ever forget.

What to drink

Champagne. It's a party, dammit.

graham cracker pie with banana and coconut

When we were growing up and he was helping build my character by beating the crap out of me every few minutes, my brother always asked for, and got, a graham cracker pie on his birthday. At least, that's how I remember it. Anyway, it's a ridiculously delicious, and ridiculously easy to make, crust. If you must, buy a box of graham cracker crumbs and use those, but I like to use whole crackers and pulverize them myself because I like pulverizing stuff. You can fill it with whatever flavor pudding you want, vanilla to chocolate to guava-ginger-lychee, but in this recipe, I'm going bananas.

Cooking spray for the pan

FOR THE CRUST

2 cups crushed **graham crackers** *(to crush, drop about 10 crackers into a Ziploc bag, then crush with a rolling pin or skillet into a coarse grain)*

½ cup *(1 stick)* **unsalted butter**, melted

⅓ cup **sugar**

1 teaspoon **ground cinnamon**

A few gratings of **nutmeg**

1 **egg white**, well beaten

FOR THE FILLING

1 cup **sugar**

1 cup **sweetened shredded coconut**

½ cup **buttermilk**

½ cup **milk**

2 tablespoons **all-purpose flour**

2 large **eggs** plus 2 **egg yolks**

1 teaspoon **pure vanilla extract**

Pinch of **salt**

1 **banana**, sliced into rounds

FOR THE BANANAS

2 tablespoons **unsalted butter**

1 tablespoon **brown sugar**

3 **bananas**, sliced in half lengthwise

FOR THE TOPPING

1 cup **heavy** *(whipping)* **cream**

2 tablespoons **powdered sugar**

continued

Preheat the oven to 350°F. Lightly spray a 9-inch pie pan with the cooking spray.

make the crust

Add the crust ingredients, except the egg white, and mix together with your hands. Press the mixture evenly into the pie pan with your fingers. Brush the egg white on all surfaces of the crust to seal it. Bake on the center rack for about 15 minutes, until golden brown. Let cool.

make the filling

In a large bowl, whisk together all the filling ingredients except the banana rounds. Lay the banana rounds in the cooled pie crust, then pour the filling over the top. Bake for 40 minutes, until it's set but still jiggles. Let cool on a wire rack to room temperature.

make the bananas

Meanwhile, melt the butter and brown sugar in a medium sauté pan. Sauté the banana slices for 3 minutes on each side, then remove from the heat. Let cool.

make the topping

Lay the sautéed bananas over the top of the pie. Beat the whipping cream and powdered sugar until the cream holds stiff peaks, about 4 minutes with a mixer, about 8 minutes by hand. Spread over the pie.

Doctor it up

Add a couple tablespoons of rum to the filling.

Serve this

On my brother's birthday. Or your brother's. Or your mother's.

What to drink

Something about banana makes me thirsty for rum drinks. Daiquiri, anyone?

it's the chocolate, stupid

So what if it's a little 1977? When it comes to love, chocolate fondue *works*. In fact, if you make this for your date and you *don't* get any action, hit the self-help section. I got nothing for you here. You'll need a fondue pot for this, which believe it or not is worth having. It'll run you about $25 for a decent good-budget fondue pot. You can use the same pot for cheese fondue, meat fondue, or certain *shabu shabu* dishes. People go nuts for it and think it's way more complicated than it is.

¾ cup **heavy** *(whipping)* **cream**

1¼ pounds good-quality **semisweet chocolate**, milk or dark, broken into small chunks

2 to 3 tablespoons **kirsch** *(or Grand Marnier, if that's your thing)*

¼ teaspoon **dried ancho chile powder**

Powdered sugar for coating

½ **lemon**

Sliced **bananas**

Whole **strawberries**

Cake donuts, cut into chunks

Prepare the fondue pot. In other words, wash the hell out of it. Chances are it's been collecting dust for a while. And if the last thing you made in there was cheese fondue, there's probably still some garlic residue in there, so scrub away.

continued

C07 Dessert

In a medium saucepan over medium heat, bring the cream to just short of a simmer—until you can just dip your finger in, but not hold it there; no bubbles. Add the chocolate and whisk slowly into the cream. Stir until melted and the color evens. Add the kirsch and chile powder, whisking slowly until the mixture appears glossy. Remove from the heat.

Light the fondue pot and add the melted chocolate mixture to the pot.

Pour a small mound of powdered sugar onto each plate. Grate the zest from the lemon over each pile of sugar. Spear the fruit and donuts in any way you like with fondue forks. Dip into the fondue to coat. Then, drop the chocolate-covered item into the lemony powdered sugar. Eat immediately.

Doctor it up

Substitute a blanched and chopped habanero pepper for the ancho powder, but keep a sweat towel handy.

Serve this

When the sheets are clean.

What to drink

A fortified dessert wine, such as a Sauternes. Or, a glass of Baileys on ice.

maple berry crisp

A great summer dessert, this switch-up on the traditional apple crisp takes advantage of what's freshest in the summer. But if you're reading this in January, don't panic. This sucker is just as good with frozen berries, any time of year.

3 cups **berries** *(blueberries, raspberries, blackberries, strawberries, etc.)*

½ cup **pure maple syrup**

1 cup **all-purpose flour**

1 cup **old-fashioned rolled oats**

½ cup firmly packed **brown sugar**

1 teaspoon **ground cinnamon**

A few gratings of **nutmeg**

½ cup *(1 stick)* cold **unsalted butter**, chopped into small pieces

Ice cream for serving

Preheat the oven to 350°F. Put the berries in a medium bowl, then pour the maple syrup over the top. Stir and set aside.

Mix together the flour, oats, brown sugar, cinnamon, and nutmeg. Quickly mix in the butter with your fingers, mashing the butter into the dry ingredients with as little contact as possible. It doesn't have to be thoroughly mixed, and you want the butter to stay cold until it cooks, so no sweaty palms. If you'd rather, you can use a pastry blender for this, but fingers are just as good.

Spoon the berries into an 8-inch square *(or 9-inch round)* baking dish or pan. Sprinkle the topping over the fruit, covering it completely. Bake for 45 minutes. Serve with ice cream.

Doctor it up

Don't like berries? Ask me if I care, and try peaches or apples or pears instead.

Serve this

On a weeknight.

What to drink

The last of that bottle of white that's been sitting in your fridge. Or, hot chocolate.

C07 Dessert

183

rum
with

Not everyone digs boozy desserts. That's fine: More for me! I love drunken desserts. This rummy cake, which tastes a little like Jamaica and a little like Georgia, should quench your inner pirate of the Caribbean. It's good in summer with a little less rum, better in winter with a little more.

Cooking spray and **flour** for the pan

½ can *(6 ounces)* **Coca-Cola**

¼ cup plus 2 tablespoons **dark** or **light rum**

1 tablespoon **white vinegar**

1 box *(about 18 ounces)* **yellow cake mix**

3 **eggs**, lightly beaten

2 tablespoons **vegetable oil**

1 can **peach halves in heavy syrup**, drained well *(save the syrup)*

2 tablespoons **powdered sugar**

1 cup **heavy** *(whipping)* **cream**

1 teaspoon **rum extract**

and coke cake
peaches

Preheat the oven to 350°F. Lightly spray a 9-by-13-inch baking pan with the cooking spray, then dust with flour. In a small bowl, mix together the Coke, the ¼ cup rum, and the vinegar. Combine the cake mix, eggs, oil, and Coke mixture in a bowl and stir until smooth.

Pour the batter into the pan. Lay the peach halves, cut-side up, on top of the batter, pressing them into the batter slightly. Bake for 30 minutes, or until a toothpick stuck in the middle comes out fairly clean.

Mix together the reserved peach syrup and the remaining 2 tablespoons rum. While the cake is still warm, poke about 20 holes in the top with a toothpick and drizzle the entire cake with this rum mixture. Let cool completely in the pan. Sprinkle with the powdered sugar. Whip the cream with the rum extract for 5 to 8 minutes, until peaks begin to form. Serve directly from the pan, with the rummy whipped cream.

Doctor it up

Not into rum? Fair enough. Use Jim Beam instead and make this a Kentucky Bourbon Cake.

Serve this

When family comes to visit. If everyone smells like booze, no one knows when you're taking secret nips on the side.

What to drink

Rum and Coke, natch.

C07 Dessert

makes one 9-inch pie

fried apple pie

You could call this a tarte Tatin if you wanted to, but then you'd have to sit there and think about how to pronounce *Tatin* without sounding like a dope. Besides, it may have French roots, but this fried pie is an all-American affair. *(You can tell by the maple.)* This calls for a frozen pie crust, but if you want to make your own, go for it. I do it sometimes, too. There are many good recipes out there for flaky, buttery pie dough, and to be honest, it's not even all that hard.

4 to 6 **Golden Delicious apples**

Juice of ½ **lemon**

½ cup *(1 stick)* **unsalted butter**

½ cup **sugar**

½ cup **pure maple syrup**, plus extra for serving

1 teaspoon **ground cinnamon**

One 9-inch **frozen pie crust**, thawed slightly *(or make your own)*

Ice cream for serving

Preheat the oven to 400°F. Peel and core the apples. Slice into eighths, lengthwise, creating little spears. You should have about 4 cups. Toss them in a bowl with the lemon juice. In a medium, ovenproof frying or sauté pan *(cast iron is best)* over medium heat, sauté the butter, sugar, maple syrup, and cinnamon until the butter begins to melt. Add the apple slices, all in one layer with as little overlap as possible. Cook for 10 minutes, then flip the apples and cook for another 5 minutes. Remove from the heat.

Drape the crust over the apples and press lightly into the pan. Slide the pan into the oven and bake for 25 minutes, or until the crust looks good and brown. Remove from the oven. Let cool in the pan on a wire rack for 20 minutes, then loosen the edges with a spatula or knife and flip the pan onto a serving plate. Carefully remove the pan. Serve warm with ice cream and a drizzle of maple, or serve cold later.

Doctor it up

Get some cranberries up in under that crust. Pears. Or maybe a little candied ginger. Pineapple? Go for it.

Serve this

Sunday supper.

What to drink

Another glass of whatever you served with dinner earlier, if there's any left. Or coffee.

The best bread pudding I ever had was at the Cashway Café in Broadus, Montana. It came with a pint of half-and-half for garnish. Theirs is the Holy Grail of bread pudding. But this one's pretty good. It's an easy recipe because unlike most bread puddings, you don't need to make a water bath to cook it in. Not that making a water bath is all that hard, but who needs it? This bread pudding is vaguely North African, in its way.

1   loaf stale **country white** or **Italian bread**, trimmed of crust and cut into ½-inch slices

2   tablespoons **unsalted butter**

3   **eggs** plus 1 **egg yolk**

3   cups **milk**

1   cup **sugar**

½   cup **honey**

2   teaspoons **pure almond extract**

2   teaspoons **ground cinnamon**

½   teaspoon **ground cardamom**

1   teaspoon ground **allspice**

   Zest of ½ **lemon**

   A few gratings of **nutmeg**

   Half-and-half for serving

spiced bread pudding

serves 6

Preheat the oven to 200°F. Halve the bread slices, then lay the slices on baking sheets and dry them in the oven for 20 minutes.

Thoroughly coat an 8-inch square baking pan with the butter. Pack bread slices tightly into the pan.

Whisk together all the remaining ingredients except the half-and-half until smooth, then pour over the bread. Let sit for 1 hour, making sure all the custard is absorbed. *(Help it along if it needs it by pushing down on it with the back of a spoon.)*

Up the oven to 375°F. Bake the pudding for 1 hour. Let cool on a wire rack. Serve in bowls with nice healthy splashes of half-and-half.

Doctor it up

Add 2 tablespoons of Scotch to the custard. Also, add dried apples in between the bread slices before baking.

Serve this

Shortly after you discover the stale bread.

What to drink

A zesty herbal tea, hit with a shot of Scotch.

index

Index

191

table of equivalents

Some of these numbers are rounded. So sue us.

Liquid/Dry Measures

U.S.	Metric
¼ teaspoon	1.25 milliliters
½ teaspoon	2.5 milliliters
1 teaspoon	5 milliliters
1 tablespoon *(3 teaspoons)*	15 milliliters
1 fluid ounce *(2 tablespoons)*	30 milliliters
¼ cup	60 milliliters
⅓ cup	80 milliliters
½ cup	120 milliliters
1 cup	240 milliliters
1 pint *(2 cups)*	480 milliliters
1 quart *(4 cups, 32 ounces)*	960 milliliters
1 gallon *(4 quarts)*	3.84 liters
1 ounce *(by weight)*	28 grams
1 pound	448 grams
2.2 pounds	1 kilogram

Lengths

U.S.	Metric
⅛ inch	3 millimeters
¼ inch	6 millimeters
½ inch	12 millimeters
1 inch	2.5 centimeters

Oven Temperatures

Fahrenheit	Celsius	Gas
250	120	½
275	140	1
300	150	2
325	160	3
350	180	4
375	190	5
400	200	6
425	220	7
450	230	8
475	240	9
500	260	10